JU-JITSU
UNLEASHED

JIU-JITSU UNLEASHED

A COMPREHENSIVE GUIDE TO THE WORLD'S HOTTEST MARTIAL ARTS DISCIPLINE

EDDIE BRAVO

with Erich Krauss

McGraw·Hill

New York   Chicago   San Francisco   Lisbon   London   Madrid   Mexico City
Milan   New Delhi   San Juan   Seoul   Singapore   Sydney   Toronto

The **McGraw·Hill** Companies

Library of Congress Cataloging-in-Publication Data

Bravo, Eddie.
    Jiu-Jitsu unleashed : a comprehensive guide to the world's hottest martial arts discipline /
Eddie Bravo with Erich Krauss.
       p.   cm.
    Includes index.
    ISBN 0-07-144811-X
    1. Jiu-jitsu.   I. Krauss, Erich, 1971-   II. Title.

GV1114.B73   2006
796.815'2—dc22   2005017827

6 7 8 9 0 DOC/DOC 0 9 8

ISBN 0-07-144811-X

This book is for educational purposes. It is not intended as a substitute for individual fitness and
health advice. Neither McGraw-Hill nor the authors shall have any responsibility for any adverse
effects arising directly or indirectly as a result of information provided in this book.

McGraw-Hill books are available at special quantity discounts to use as premiums and sales
promotions, or for use in corporate training programs. For more information, please write to the
Director of Special Sales, Professional Publishing, McGraw-Hill, Two Penn Plaza, New York, NY
10121-2298. Or contact your local bookstore.

This book is printed on acid-free paper.

Contents

Foreword

Martial arts have been around for thousands of years, but for some reason most styles of martial arts have improved very little in that time. When you walk into a traditional karate or kung fu school today, you're very likely to be taught the same techniques that were used back when Columbus was sailing.

Now, the world of jiu-jitsu is very different than most traditional martial arts in that you can trace a very distinct evolution in the art back to the Gracie family in Brazil. It's very clear that the contributions of Carlos and Helio Gracie, along with all of their sons and students, have forever changed the concepts we had of hand-to-hand combat. They took an existing martial art and advanced it far past its roots into the most complete and effective form of fighting known to

man—what we now know as Brazilian jiu-jitsu.

There are many people who have learned this style and became very good at it, but few have actually contributed to the evolution of the art. There are a few who add something; a particular sweep that they've invented, a new way to get a certain collar choke . . . but even with the most innovative guys, it usually involves just one or two moves that are attributed to them. Most of what is in their game are the same techniques everyone else is using.

And that is what's so special about my good friend Eddie Bravo. He has invented so many techniques and improved upon so many traditional moves that he has literally created a completely separate style of jiu-jitsu.

Eddie is an incredibly creative guy, easily one of the most creative people

I've ever met in my life. His main outlet for that creativity most of his life has been music. He makes very cool electronica-style music, and one of the more interesting things about Eddie's music is that he is involved in every aspect of it. He's not just a musician who does one thing well, such as playing the guitar or the drums. He actually writes and edits the music and plays all the instruments. Now there are a lot of musicians out there, but there are very few who can do *everything*. Even fewer can do it and have those songs actually be cool to listen to.

It takes a very special kind of brain to get good at all those facets of music, and actually have the creativity to combine all those skills and come up with something your ears and your mind lock on to. Now what's *really* rare, is to take someone who has that very special kind of creative mind, and have them plug that same unusual thought process into coming up with new ways to strangle people. It usually just doesn't happen.

Most musicians are just concentrating on making their music, and during their time off they're partying. Very few of them have the discipline to become really good at grappling with people and getting them to submit just with their bare hands, and even

fewer have the inspiration or the ability to come up with new ways to do it. It's a very, very rare situation.

With this unusual combination of an incredibly creative mind combined with a passion for submitting people, Eddie has come up with a very unique approach to martial arts. If you've never seen him fight and aren't familiar with his moves, you will be completely lost as to what he's doing to you, right until the point where you tap out. I've seen it firsthand many, many times during the years that I've known him. Tough guys with years and years of grappling experience who spar with him wind up twisted in knots with a confused look on their faces, completely baffled as to what's going on.

His approach is so innovative and so unusual that it literally is a completely separate branch of the jiu-jitsu tree. And it's not just different—it's actually better. *Much* better.

Another thing that makes Eddie so special is that he's willing to share these innovations completely and without reservation with anyone who will listen. What took him years and years to develop and refine, can now be yours. In this book, he allows you to cut through all the trial and error that he had to go through to develop these techniques and gives you his exact thought process through every aspect of them. He provides not just ways to submit people, but entire paths to get there.

What you are about to read in *Jiu-Jitsu Unleashed* is, in my opinion, the future of the art of jiu-jitsu. Years from now the techniques you see on these pages won't just be different or optional, they'll be standard. They'll be what all the competitors will use, not because they're new techniques or because you can catch people off guard with them, but because they're truly the best techniques, especially for jiu-jitsu without the gi.

We're very lucky to have a guy like Eddie in the world of martial arts, and even luckier that he's willing to teach what he knows. I truly believe that when all is said and done, this book will become one of the most important books ever written on martial arts. So buckle up, strap yourself in, and prepare to absorb Eddie Bravo's very own 10th Planet Jiu-Jitsu in *Jiu-Jitsu Unleashed: A Comprehensive Guide to the World's Hottest Martial Arts Discipline.*

JOE ROGAN,
host of NBC's "Fear Factor"

Acknowledgments

First and foremost I want to thank from the bottom of my heart, my master, Jean Jacques Machado. He is the one who guided me along this path of ever evolving jiu-jitsu. He was the one who made me realize what confidence really is and just how crucial it is for success not only in jiu-jitsu but life as well. He was the only one who was there time and time again to help me break through the roadblocks of jiu-jitsu.

I would also like to thank my two best friends, Joe Rogan and Laurence Zwirn.

Joe, for being the first to call me a phenom, for giving me my first computer, for my hernia surgery, for forcing my talent down people's throats, for making me laugh harder than any other person on the planet, for the thousands of meals, and for just being the best friend anyone can ever hope for. Joe rules.

Laurence, for buying all my mats, for constantly hooking me up with girls, for the thousand meals, for the crazy times in Vegas, for the lifetime supply of supplements (Nature's Purest *rules*), for all the financial help you have given me, and for just chillin' day in and day out. Ehhhahhhh!!!!!!!

A very special thanks goes out to the Gracie family. Though we have different views on the gi, I do appreciate tremendously what you did for the world of martial arts and my world.

Thank you Helio for being the warrior and innovator that you are. Who has tougher sons than you? No one.

Thank you Carlos Sr. for taking in the Machados as sons of your own and introducing them to the fascinating world of jiu-jitsu.

Thank you Rorion for producing the UFC; without you the MMA industry would not exist and I would be still deejaying in clubs.

Thank you Royce for having the courage to step up and fight in eight- and sixteen-man tournaments just to prove the effectiveness of jiu-jitsu. You will always be a legend.

Thank you Rickson for being the superman of the jiu-jitsu world. There is no one I would rather see in the ring than you.

And thank you Royler for being you. Without you and your unbelievable accomplishments in the grappling world, this book would not exist.

A very special thank-you to Larry Goldberg for being the most crucial piece of my literary career.

And last but not least, a very special thank-you to my top student, Gerald "The Finishing Machine" Strebendt, for believing in me and my techniques and for being my MMA prototype to prove to the world the effectiveness of 10th Planet Jiu-Jitsu.

A special thanks also goes out to Glen Cordoza, who spent hundreds of hours on the mats and behind the computer helping to write this book. If not for your talent as a writer, fighter, and loyal friend, this book could not have been written.

About This Book

In 2003 I entered the Abu Dhabi World Championships, the largest and most respected no-gi grappling tournament in the world, and tapped out Royler Gracie, the most accomplished jiu-jitsu player in the world-renowned Gracie family. I managed such a feat not because I'm a jiu-jitsu phenom born to grapple, but because I did what no one else dared to try—broke jiu-jitsu down and developed a system that didn't require holding on to your opponent's uniform for control or submissions.

In traditional Brazilian jiu-jitsu, the gi has almost become a holy garment. Players use the collar and sleeve of their opponent's uniform to set up submissions, sweeps, and passes. This works wonderfully for regular grappling tournaments where competitors wear a gi, but it does not translate well for no-gi grappling tournaments or mixed martial arts (MMA) competitions such as the Ultimate Fighting Championship (UFC). If a traditional jiu-jitsu player who bases all his techniques on holding on to his opponent's uniform steps into a ring or cage with a competitor who is not wearing a uniform, he immediately loses all of his offensive setups. He is forced to play defense, and this often costs him the fight.

I did not want to have to relearn jiu-jitsu or break a bunch of bad gi habits if I one day decided to enter MMA competition, so in 1996 I started developing a system of jiu-jitsu that was not based on the gi, testing each technique in competition before permanently adding it to my game. It is a system that you will find nowhere else but in this book. What I have laid out on the following pages is not a random pile of moves. Each chapter is linked to the next, and each technique is described in detail through narrative and step-by-step photos. There are no hidden steps. There are no moves that haven't been proven time and again in the highest levels of competition. Unlike most jiu-jitsu black belt instructors, I am not afraid of divulging my secrets. Perhaps this will come back to haunt me in competition, but sharing all my knowledge is the only way I know how to teach.

So if you want to learn a style of jiu-jitsu that is MMA- and street-ready, I suggest you read on. Whether you are a beginner or an advanced player, I also suggest that you start with Chapter 1 and the half guard, which is exactly where I started. Once you have a good grasp of the half guard, move to the next chapter, which is the full guard. By the time you have mastered all the techniques in this book, you'll have a leg up on nearly all traditional jiu-jitsu players in no-gi grappling tournaments and MMA competition. While your opponent is busy searching for the collar and sleeve that isn't there, you'll land submissions utilizing over-hooks, under-hooks, and head control.

You'll also begin to see that I haven't thought of everything, that despite what traditional black belt jiu-jitsu instructors want you to believe, jiu-jitsu is still evolving. Just like my current students, you'll start coming up with techniques on your own. And, as you do, you will understand that it's the *grappling* that makes jiu-jitsu the most dominant martial art in the world, not the uniform.

Introduction

My Evolution

Shortly after moving to Hollywood in 1991, I signed a two-year contract at a local health club. As a twenty-year-old singer and guitarist in a rock band that was going to make it big time, I didn't want to be standing up on stage looking like a slob. But despite all my good intentions, I only went twice. I paid the monthly dues each and every month, yet I only went twice in two whole years. After spending the majority of high school hiding in the shadows while the rest of the wrestling team hit the weight room, I should have known that I despised pumping iron.

I still wanted to get into shape, so I put the brain to work, asking myself what I could possibly do to lose a few pounds, and then Bruce Lee sprang to mind. He was the toughest man on the planet—ripped to the bone—so I decided to take some kind of karate or kung fu. I didn't know much about the Eastern martial arts, which style was the most deadly, so I opened the phone book, got the address of the closest school, and then headed down there.

The instructor's name was Professor Phillip Skornia, and within five minutes I became certain he could kill anyone with a single strike. He had a black belt in everything—aikido, judo, tae kwon do, shorin-ryu karate, five-animal kung fu. He was even some kind of ordained monk at the Shaolin Temple. I remember thinking, "Oh my God, the stars must be aligned! There were over fifty schools I could have chosen from, and I picked the ultimate one!"

So I ended up studying Zen Du Ru Karate, which means "the style of inner strength," or something like that. It was Professor Skornia's very own style. He had taken the best moves from each of the disciplines he'd mastered through the years and combined them into the most savage martial art. After six months, I had a green stripe on my white belt and had become a master at the overhand knife strike. Professor Skornia had even acknowledged my prowess when I'd taken my test, writing "Excellent overhand knife strike" on my grade sheet. Needless to say, I felt pretty confident.

I brought that confidence with me when I went back home to Orange County, California, just a few hours south of Hollywood, to attend an Alice 'n Chains concert with a few of my high school buddies. I hadn't seen them in a couple of years, and on the way to the concert they were acting funny, shooting me strange glances.

"What's going on?" I eventually asked.

"We heard you were doing that karate stuff," one of them said, almost in awe.

"Yeah, I've been doing that for a little while now, bro."

"You must be able to kick some ass, right?"

"Yeah," I said. "I've been training for like six months."

I ate it up. Even though I only weighed 160 pounds, I was certain that I could beat anyone other than Professor Skornia in a fight. As it turned out, my friends thought that too, and they wanted to see me in action. While at the concert, I went upstairs to use the restroom. When I came out, all my friends were standing there, shuffling from side to side, sweat beading their brows. They'd been looking all over for me. Apparently there was some guy down on the floor, shoving women, giving everyone a hard time.

"We were going to confront him," one of my friends said, "but we thought we'd find you first."

I didn't feel the surge of panic one usually feels before a confrontation because at that time I truly thought Zen Du Ru practitioners such as myself were invincible. "Show me," I said. "Show me where he is."

They all pointed down to the crowd on the first floor, and I led the way with my shoulders puffed out. As we walked down the stairs, I kept thinking, "Should I use my reverse punch or my overhand knife strike?" After much inner debate, I decided to go with the overhand knife strike. I would tell the brute to stop pushing on people, to leave without a fight. Once he disobeyed, I would walk up, get into position, and then *ka-chop*!

Thank God we never found him. I mean, come on, who is just going to stand there while I gather my chi for an overhand knife strike? He would have punched me square in the nose and I would have gone down. The incident would have become one of those painful stories that my friends always bring up when we get together every five years. I can just see it, all of them rolling around with laugher, chopping ridiculously at the air while I sleek off to some corner in shame. I would have been hearing about how I got my butt kicked in a karate stance until the day I died.

The only good that could have come out of getting my butt kicked is that I would have realized sooner that I was being scammed, taken for a serious ride. I still hadn't learned that yet, so I continued with perfecting my overhand knife strike. I really got into karate, but because they didn't have televised karate tournaments, I watched the next best thing, which was boxing. I became a boxing fanatic. Although I rehearsed with my band every night of the week, I would tape "Tuesday Night Fights" on the USA Network. When I popped one such tape into the VCR back in 1993, I saw a commercial for the Ultimate Fighting Championship (UFC). They didn't have any highlights because it was the first event, so instead they showed a karate guy sparring with a kung fu guy in a gym. They kept saying, "The

Ultimate Fighting Championship, NO RULES FIGHTING!"

A few of my friends wanted to order it on pay per view, but I talked them out of it. I thought it was some type of pro wrestling and that everything was going to be fake. The event passed without any of us seeing it, but then one day a friend came to my house totally out of breath. It looked like he had run several miles.

"Dude, you know that Ultimate Challenge thing," he said, huffing and puffing.

"Yeah."

"Dude, it was real!"

"It was real?"

"Yeah. There was some Iranian guy, and he was choking people out. He was just grabbing their tracheas and their throats, and he was squeezing their necks."

"Some Iranian guy is grabbing people's throats?" I asked.

"Yeah, he was choking everyone out, man. That's what the guy was telling me at Guitar Center."

"No way," I said. "Was there a karate guy in there?"

"Yeah, he beat all styles. He beat kung fu, everybody."

"Not karate," I said.

"Yeah, he beat a karate guy, too."

"No way, that is my style. Karate is the best."

I couldn't believe it. No matter how many people told me what had happened at the event, I still couldn't believe it. I was brainwashed, so I put it out of my mind and continued learning from the professor. Approximately six months later, as I was getting ready to go to a party, a friend called up and said UFC 2 was on that night. I told him to order it and tape it. By that time, I'd heard the name Royce Gracie at least a hundred times, and I considered it a personal assault on my style and my professor. I wanted to see what this jiu-jitsu stuff was all about.

The next morning I ended up watching UFC 2 on tape. Gracie, a 180-pound Brazilian, was the bad guy. I wanted him to lose. I wanted him to get his head knocked off. I hoped it would be a karate guy that did it, but at that point it didn't really matter. I just wanted him to lose so that his name would go away. So when he fought Minoki Ichihara, a traditional karate practitioner from Japan, I found myself screaming, "Come on Ichihara, beat him up. Kick his ass, karate!" But by the time Gracie stepped into the finals to face Patrick Smith, a tae kwon do practitioner who looked more like a street brawler, my loathing toward the Brazilian had completely vanished. I could see that he was the real deal, and

I found myself wanting to know the same thinigs he knew. After all, I had wrestled for two years in high school and it seemed somewhat similar to this submission stuff. Immediately I began thinking about the Twister (see Chapter 3), the only move I had walked away with after two years on the wrestling mats.

Feeling I might be good at grappling, I did the unthinkable. One afternoon after training with Professor Skornia, I hopped into my car and drove to a jiu-jitsu school. The instructor let me hang around and watch class, but within a few minutes I noticed that they weren't doing the same thing Gracie had done in the Octagon at the UFC. Other than executing some funky rolls that looked like something you might see in a Ninja movie, they spent hardly any time on the ground. And they wore black uniforms. That really bothered me, the black uniforms. They should be wearing white uniforms just like Gracie. I began looking around, wondering what was going on here, and I noticed from a sign on the wall that they weren't doing jiu-jitsu at all, but rather *jujutsu*. I didn't see how a one-letter difference in the name could change things all that much, but apparently it did.

"What did you think?" the instructor asked after class.

"Why aren't you guys doing that much ground work?" I asked, but what I really wanted to ask was *How come you guys are wearing black uniforms?*

"You must be thinking of that Gracie jiu-jitsu stuff."

"Isn't this the same thing?"

"No. That is mostly ground work. We only spend about 15 percent of the time on the ground. But Gracie's cousins, the Machados, have a school out here in LA. I could get you their number."

"No, no," I said, not wanting to offend him. "I don't want to do that other stuff, I want to do this stuff." But the whole time we were talking, I kept thinking to myself *Machado, Machado, Machado—don't forget—Machado, Machado.*

So I took his paperwork knowing that I would never come back. An hour later, I called information, got the address of the Machado Academy, and headed over there. I was so excited when I walked through the door I could hardly contain myself. But that excitement quickly drained away when I found out how much it cost to be a student at the Machado Academy. It was $125 a month! I didn't have $125, so I left. Karate had been shattered in my eyes, and with the secrets of Brazilian jiu-jitsu too expensive to afford, I decided to study Jeet Kune Do, the style of the only man who still seemed tougher than Gracie—Bruce Lee.

I did that for six months, working on kicks and punches, and then I landed a job as a DJ at a nightclub. For the first time since I'd come to Hollywood, I finally had some money in my pocket. I liked what I was learning in Jeet Kune Do, so instead of quitting, I decided to splurge and start taking jiu-jitsu from the Machados as well. Doing both would make me a complete warrior. I would have punches and kicks for the initial flurry, and if things weren't going my way, I could take my opponent down and finish him off with a submission.

I kept it up for two and a half years, spending every Tuesday and Thursday on stand-up and Friday on the ground. But my dream of becoming the complete warrior didn't materialize as I had hoped. Grappling just one day a week wasn't enough to get me anywhere. The new guys who were training five days a week would be able to tap me out after just a few months of training. That's when I decided to quit training stand-up, pick it up at a later date, and dedicate all my time to working on jiu-jitsu.

I became obsessed, but according to Jean Jacques Machado, I wasn't obsessed with the right stuff. During practice, I kept going for the Twister. I tried to tell him that it was a wrestling move, but he didn't believe me. He thought I had made it up. "You have to start learning basic jiu-jitsu," he said to me one day. "Your basic jiu-jitsu is terrible. You keep trying this crazy Twister thing. You already know that. Now you must start expanding your game. You have to start playing regular jiu-jitsu."

I listened to what he had to say, but I didn't give up on the Twister. In wrestling, it was an easy move to execute because people were always giving me their backs. No one gave me their backs in jiu-jitsu, not by choice anyway, so I knew that in order to make it work I would have to find some other way to slap it on. I learned it was easier to get an opponent in side control than taking his back, so that's when I came up with a Twister setup from side control. By the time I became a blue belt, I was catching guys with the Twister all the time. Instead of doing it off traditional side control, however, I did it off this new and improved side control position I'd come up with, which I named Twister Side Control. I realized that my basic

jiu-jitsu still stunk, but I also realized that many of the basic moves wouldn't work for me. I still hated lifting weights, so I wasn't all that strong. Every time I went for guillotines, kimuras, leg locks, or toeholds, my opponent would simply power out of them and then toss me around. In order to make those moves work, I figured I had to be just as strong as my opponent, if not stronger. So instead I focused on little man moves, such as the rear naked choke. Even a 220-pound muscle-bound practitioner can't power out of a rear naked choke, not once you have it locked in. It just didn't make sense to me to practice moves that were only going to work on a weaker opponent, especially because I was one of the weakest guys in the gym.

Despite my reluctance to follow the traditional path, jiu-jitsu became the center of my universe. I watched every UFC, and each time a jiu-jitsu practitioner stepped into the infamous Octagon to do battle, I'd slap my friend in the chest and point to the television. "Watch this," I'd say. "The jiu-jitsu guy is going to have his opponent screaming in pain in a matter of minutes." Most of the time it worked out just that way, which fueled my confidence that traditional jiu-jitsu was the ultimate fighting style on the planet. But then, as the years began to pass, the jiu-jitsu players entering the UFC stopped being such an opposing force. They still took their opponents to the ground, and they still captured their opponents between their legs in the guard, but then they would just lie there, defending against punches. Their inactivity had nothing to do with their skill level. It had to do with the fact that every kickboxer and wrestler in the event had learned just enough jiu-jitsu to avoid getting caught in submissions. Back when Gracie had first stepped into the event, he'd had it easy. No one knew how to defend against chokeholds or arm bars, and he'd cleaned house. That just wasn't the case anymore.

I thought it would only be a matter of time before my fellow jiu-jitsu players competing in the UFC began changing their game to adapt to this new development. But they never did. They continued to just lie there, holding on to their opponent while trying to avoid punches. Just as I began to wonder if perhaps jiu-jitsu *wasn't* the best fighting style on the planet, it dawned on me why they were having so much trouble. It wasn't that they didn't know how to grapple, but rather that they didn't know how to grapple when their opponent wasn't wearing a gi. They had based all their setups, submissions, passes, and sweeps off holding on to their opponent's collar and sleeve. If their opponent didn't have a sleeve or collar to grab, all their techniques went right out the window.

It made perfect sense. In order to land submissions in a no-gi tournament, you had to practice jiu-jitsu techniques that didn't require holding on to your opponent's uniform. Nearly all the jiu-jitsu competitors competing in mixed martial arts (MMA) latched on to their opponents' arms using over-hooks for defense, but then they would let go of the over-hooks to go for a submission and take the risk of getting punched in the face. It only seemed logical for them to learn how to submit to their opponents while maintaining the over-hook control because then they would not only be in a defensive position, but an offensive one as well.

I suggested this strategy to a few of my fellow jiu-jitsu practitioners, and they nearly bit my head off. How dare I suggest something as ludicrous as learning how to grapple without the gi? They were brainwashed like the rest of the jiu-jitsu world, but that didn't stop me from continuing with my plans. My intention wasn't to develop my own style. I didn't want to be the guy inventing his own moves. But with 99 percent of the jiu-jitsu schools teaching moves based on the gi, it began to look more and more as if that was what I would have to do. As it turned out, I didn't have to go far to get the help I needed to do that.

My instructor, Jean Jacques, was 50 percent better than most of the traditional jiu-jitsu instructors when it came to techniques that didn't require holding on to the gi. It wasn't that he was against wearing a uniform; he wore one all the time. He was 50 percent better because he had no fingers on his left hand. He couldn't grab the collar or sleeve of his opponent's uniform with that hand, so he would use it to secure an over-hook. That's part of the reason he blew through the competition in the late 1990s when he began entering these big competitions. Even though Jean Jacques still played the traditional game with his right hand, gripping at his opponent's collar, I could see just how much the tactics he employed with his left hand had helped him in these no-gi tournaments. I was going to follow his lead, only I wasn't going to grab my opponent's uniform with either hand. That way, when I began entering these big competitions, I would be 100 percent

more prepared than those who had been training with the gi, which was just about everyone.

Jean Jacques guided me through the process; as a result, his fingerprints are all over my style. I might have carved my own way, doing what no one else was doing at the time by developing a highly individualistic style based on no-gi techniques. But without Jean Jacques's help, I never would have been able to put it all together. He helped me figure out the best movements in every no-gi position. He helped me decide where to place my hands for defense and how my legs should get involved. He helped me put every limb to work so that while I was defending against punches I could still be going for a submission. We went through many frustrating years trying to reinvent the wheel, but it began to pay off. I started smoking people in the gym, getting one submission after the next. It gave me a sense of accomplishment, but the ultimate test would be to see how it held up in competition.

The Proving Ground

They're pretty much the same animal: competition and real fighting. Standing out in the street just before a fight, you feel the same stress you do when standing in a warm-up room prior to a tournament. You get a sinking sensation in your gut, your mouth dries up, and your palms begin to sweat. I wasn't looking forward to those feelings, but I knew that if I ever wanted my style of jiu-jitsu to work out in the street or in MMA competition, I had to get used to the pressure. Slapping a new technique on someone in the gym and making him tap was easy. It was much harder to slap that same technique on someone who has his pride riding on the line in a competition. I knew it was going to be the ultimate proving ground because one way or another I would walk away not only knowing if I had what it took, but also if the style I had been developing was worth a damn.

Two years after I had first walked into Jean Jacques's Academy in April 1996, I entered my first jiu-jitsu competition, which was held at a police academy near Dodgers Stadium in LA. I was a blue belt at the time, and I smoked through my first two opponents. Because I hadn't taken my instructor's advice to train in the basic moves, all I really knew how to do was capture my opponent in my half guard, establish the Lockdown, flip my opponent over with an Old School

sweep, and then hold him down on the mat until time ran out. (See Chapter 1.) It had worked so well that I decided to try the same thing in the finals with Jack McVicker, who is a black belt now. But he had been watching me all afternoon and had caught on to my technique. Once I secured him in my half guard, he blocked all my sweeps. He just smothered me for an entire six minutes. Neither one of us scored a point, but because he had been on top the whole time, the judges gave him the decision. Rigan Machado, who refereed the match, seemed disappointed. Never before had he seen such a boring match.

It went on like that for some time. In the gym I was on fire, catching people in my infamous Twister submission and making them yelp, but when I entered a competition I turned into a tamed beast. I played everything cautious, never putting myself out on the limb, so rarely did I catch anyone in my homemade submissions. Then one day I just snapped. I got sick of watching myself on videotape, holding my opponent in my half guard. My friends had heard what an animal I'd become, but when they came to watch me in tournaments they wondered why I would just lay on my back the whole time without trying to do anything. I convinced myself that if the Twister worked in the gym, there was no reason why it shouldn't work in competition. I just had to find the courage to pull it off.

I found that courage at a competition I entered in Santa Cruz, California. I was grappling with my opponent, doing the same boring thing I always did, and then suddenly I went for the Twister. To my surprise, I caught him instantly. With his spine cranked out of whack, he began pounding his hand in submission. It was such a high that I used it again and again in competition, and it always blew my mind that no one ever caught on. It wasn't some superhuman submission. It was just a move that I had learned in high school wrestling with an added twist.

With some victories under my belt, Jean Jacques and I decided it was time to take it to the next level and I entered the Relson Gracie Tournament in Hawaii. Aggressive attacks had worked for me as of late, so I decided to stick with that mind-set. After beating my first opponent with a triangle choke (see Chapter 2) and my second opponent with a Kamikaze Calf Crank (see Chapter 1), I found myself in the finals. I was told to come back in an hour for the final match, but before I made it out the door the promoter

flagged me down. He told me a contestant had came late and that in order to make it into the finals I had to fight the guy. I was about to argue and tell him that I was in fact already in the finals, but then I caught sight of the new arrival. He was a gangly little kid I thought I could beat in my sleep. I told the promoter that I accepted the challenge.

My opponent was Regan Penn, B. J. Penn's brother. Although B.J. would soon make big waves in the UFC by laying siege to nearly every opponent he stepped into the Octagon with, I hadn't a clue that he or his brother were jiu-jitsu phenoms. The first second on the mat, Regan was all over me like a cheap suit. I had thought I could beat him because he looked so harmless, and here he was cranking my limbs in every which direction. I knew toeholds were illegal in the competition, but I was desperate and decided to go for one anyway. And I got it, and I held it. Just as Regan was about to tap, the referee jumped into the mix screaming about the illegal move. He told me to let go of the hold, and I did. A moment later Regan jumped on me and used the collar of my gi to lock in a choke.

Despite the loss, Jean Jacques thought I was ready to upgrade to a purple belt. I wasn't so sure I liked the idea. I had been doing well as a blue belt, and now I would be going against more experienced competitors. As I had feared, once I got my purple belt I fell back into my cautious mode in competition. Every time I climbed onto the mat, I thought I was so outmatched that survival became my only goal. This went on for a year or two, and then I realized just as I had before that these guys weren't that good, that if a blue belt could fall victim to my moves, then so could a purple belt. As a matter of fact, I realized this right in the middle of a match. I only had two minutes left to do something, so I went from half guard to full guard, crawled my legs up my opponent's back, and set up the arm bar. Just as I captured it, time ran out.

Because I hadn't done anything up until the last two minutes, my opponent won on points. That frustrated me because I knew if I had only been aggressive earlier, I would have won for sure. Shortly after that bout, which took place in 1999, I promised myself that from that point on, I would never again be timid. It didn't matter who I faced on the mat, what his reputation was. I was going to turn myself into a monster.

While running the gauntlet, I kept an eye on MMA competition. I had been certain that it was only a matter of time before competitors in the larger competitions, such as Pride and the UFC, would begin to realize what I had already realized—that spending all their time training with the gi was hurting them. But they didn't. They continued to train with the gi, and when they entered MMA competition they continued to flounder on their backs, lost without the sleeve or collar to use for setups. Without fast-paced action on the ground, many MMA fans began to lose patience with the Brazilian ground game. If too many fans began to complain, promoters would start implementing stand-up rules. That would completely change the game. Kickboxers would no longer have to learn how to grapple. All they would need to do is hold on for thirty seconds once the fight went to the ground, and then the referee would stand them back up. Then MMA competition would become nothing more than a glorified "tough man" competition. Instead of implementing stand-up rules, promoters needed to showcase grappling, because that is what makes MMA so special. But in order to do that, competitors first had to learn how to make jiu-jitsu work without the gi.

I grew so worried about the sport of MMA dying that I began posting instructional pictures of my Rubber

Guard (see Chapter 2) on the Internet, begging competitors to take a look. It just seemed to work a whole lot better than what I was seeing in MMA competition. But my efforts did no good. Every time I tuned into an event, jiu-jitsu players were getting worse and worse fighting from the guard position. A prime example was the UFC bout between Matt Hughes and Jorge Pereira, a Rickson Gracie black belt. Pereira was one of the best jiu-jitsu practitioners on the planet, but once he had Hughes in his guard all he did was lay there. He used over-hooks to block the punches, but he didn't seem to know any submissions off the over-hooks. The result was devastating—Hughes smashed him into oblivion.

After doing an ample amount of preaching on exactly what MMA jiu-jitsu practitioners were doing wrong, it dawned on me that although I had spent all my time in the gym perfecting the no-gi grappling technique, I had never put those techniques to the test in a no-gi tournament. As a matter of fact, everyone I had grappled with up to that point had been wearing a gi. I came to the conclusion that if people were ever going to listen to what I had to say, I had to have some proof. So in 1999 I began to enter no-gi tournaments, and in 2000 I entered Grappler's Quest, the largest no-gi grappling tournament in the United States. I still hadn't finished inventing my Rubber Guard, but I had done enough to have an advantage over all of my opponents, who had trained solely with the gi. I won the tournament, and it made me realize that I had been heading down the right road all of these years.

But I still didn't fully realize what I had stumbled upon—not until I began giving Joe Rogan, host of NBC's "Fear Factor," private lessons and teaching him my Rubber Guard. After our third session, he turned to me and said, "Dude, do you realize that you are a phenom?"

"What are you talking about?" I said, thinking he was busting my chops. "I'm no phenom. B. J. Penn, he's a phenom."

"No dude, you're a phenom. You're coming up with some revolutionary moves."

I still couldn't believe it. I'd never looked at myself as anything special because I had always been so offensive-minded. If I made a mistake and got caught in a submission, I wasn't good at getting out of it. That was just never my forte. My forte was turning on the heat and making my opponents tap. I was kind of like boxer Terry Norris. He was knocking people out all the time because he took chances, but by taking chances he opened himself up for shots and would get knocked out himself from time to time. I figured that in order to be a phenom, you had to be more like boxer Pernell Whitaker. He wasn't knocking anyone out, but he also didn't get knocked out himself. For him, it was defense first. I guess all the times I took chances in the gym and got caught had led me to believe I wasn't all that good. I'd seen B. J. Penn train a few times, and he never got tapped. But after hearing Rogan tell me over and over just how lethal my style was, I began to think that perhaps there was something to it after all. Perhaps a weak, 155-pound wanna-be rock star from Orange County could make it to the big time. That's when I first locked my sights on Abu Dhabi, the largest, most respected no-gi grappling tournament in the world.

2003 Abu Dhabi Qualifiers

The more I focused on perfecting the Rubber Guard and other no-gi techniques, the more I felt myself separate from the rest of the crowd. I figured I had a leg up on traditional jiu-jitsu practitioners, at least when it came to

no-gi competition, so I decided to train for the Abu Dhabi World Championships. I was going to prove once and for all that the gi was not some sacred garment. Jiu-jitsu wasn't about what you wore; it was about the movement you executed.

It was a big jump, going from Grappler's Quest to Abu Dhabi. I got nervous just thinking about it because everything surrounding the tournament seemed mysterious. It had been founded by Sheik Tahoon, a prince from Abu Dhabi. He had gone to college in San Diego and studied jiu-jitsu under Nelson Monteiro. At the time no one knew he was a billionaire; they just thought he was a Muslim guy becoming very good at jiu-jitsu. But when he headed back home, he paid a healthy sum of money to Renzo Gracie, Shawn Alvarez, and a number of other top jiu-jitsu players to join him and open up a school. Not long after that, he decided to start his own tournament. As would be expected of a sheik, it was not a small event. He flew in all the top MMA stars, Olympic wrestlers, and world champion jiu-jitsu and judo players from around the world to partake in the largest and most prestigious no-gi grappling tournament in modern times. It was like the *Enter the Dragon* of submission wrestling.

Traditionally the events were held every year in Abu Dhabi, but after 9/11 promoters turned it into a traveling show because they worried about competitors not wanting to come to the Middle East. It was decided that it would be held in the only other logical place, the birthplace of modern day jiu-jitsu—Brazil. That suited me just fine. I couldn't think of anything better than beating all the Brazilians on their home turf. I got overly excited, daydreaming about what it would be like. But I also knew that getting there would not be easy. Before I could qualify for the event, I first had to win the North American trials.

I had a lot riding on the line. About a year prior, the promoter from King of the Cage, a popular MMA competition, began taking jiu-jitsu lessons at Jean Jacques's Academy. We began talking one day after class, and I told him that if he needed someone to conduct post-fight interviews, I was his man. I went to his office the next day, and I left with the job. To show how appreciative I was, I began going to his house every Saturday to give him private lessons. Each time, I brought a slew of videotapes of MMA competitions from all over the world, giving him a blow-by-blow description of the action going on. After a few weeks of this, he asked me if I wanted to be a commentator at his events. I told him I didn't know anything about commentating, and that if I took the job I was going to call it like I saw it. In my mind, I saw it as the perfect opportunity to talk about all the flaws of traditional jiu-jitsu in MMA.

The promoter agreed to my stipulations, and for the next several shows I went off on my spiel about how practicing for MMA while wearing a gi was killing the sport. No one knew if I was the real deal—if I even knew anything about jiu-jitsu at all—so I garnered a fair share of critics. I knew that if I lost in the trials, those who had been listening to what I had to say would blow me off as a lunatic. People would also begin wondering why someone who couldn't win the North American Abu Dhabi Trials was sitting in the commentating booth at King of the Cage, and there was a high probability that I would lose my job.

But if I won, it would prove that I was right. So I tried to ignore the pressure as best I could and trained hard. Then, on October 5, 2002, I went down to San Diego and mentally prepared myself for the toughest tournament of my life, the North American

Abu Dhabi Trials. I hadn't been there for ten minutes when this guy who trained under Matt Hume, a famous MMA trainer, began talking trash. His name was Mark Ashton, and he had some mouth.

"We're going to be the first fight in the tournament," he said. "I'm going to blaze right through you. You won't even last two minutes."

"I don't know, I think you're underestimating my defense," I said. "My jiu-jitsu is pretty tight. I think I'll be able to survive at least three minutes on the mats with you. Maybe even four."

I guess the guy didn't like me playing along, because he continued to say just how badly he was going to destroy me. As he was jabbering away, I saw Alan Teo, who was one of the favorites in the event, walk past. I kept my eye on him, trying to size him up.

"You don't need to worry about Alan Teo," Ashton said. "I have to worry about Alan Teo because you won't make it past me."

"You're probably right," I said, growing tired of him. "Since we're going to be fighting each other in a couple of minutes, why don't we warm up together?"

I never thought he would go for it because it was such a crazy idea. Who would warm up with an opponent they were going to face in less than ten minutes? I had never heard of anything like that before, and I was half-kidding. But he thought it was a great idea, so we hit the mat.

I just jumped on him. I swept the hell out of him and caught him in an array of arm bars. Then I took his back and choked him. I basically did whatever I wanted by utilizing the system I had devised, and you could imagine what that did for my confidence. Just as we were winding down, the promoter came into the warm-up room and called our names.

I could tell Ashton was nervous when we got out there, and I knew that I could beat him at any moment. But I didn't want to just beat him, not after the way he had talked. I wanted to catch him in the Twister to give everyone watching a demonstration of my style. I had heard that they'd made spine locks illegal, even though heel hooks are ten times more dangerous. I hadn't brought it up in the rules meeting, and, thankfully, they hadn't said anything about it. I figured I would just slap it on, and if the referee pulled us apart, so be it. So that is what I did. I got Ashton in the Twister, just like that. As I started cranking his head, the referee shouted, "Spine lock, spine lock. You must release the hold!" The same thing had happened to me when I caught Regan Penn in a toehold, and after I'd been forced to release the hold, Penn had jumped on me and caught me in a choke. This time, however, I had come prepared. Because I had been doing the Twister so much in competition, I'd invented several transitions I could move directly into if the Twister didn't work out, and I used one of those moves now. I took Ashton's back and then sunk in a rear naked choke. The boy who had been so certain he'd beat me within two minutes tapped his hand in submission.

Ashton tried to save face after we got off the mats. He told me that things would have been different if we had met in an MMA competition, and I told him he was right. I said I would have kicked his butt in the ring instead of on the mat. He tried to say more, but I didn't have time for it. If I was going to go to Brazil, I had to focus on my next match, which was against the Canadian champion.

The kid was twice as strong as I was, but I just played my game. Immediately I pulled half guard and then swept him. Although the Twister was an illegal move, I planned to catch him in it, show everyone that I could tap him out if I wished, and then let him

go. My plan was to catch and release him like a sea bass. So after I swept him, I went for the Twister. He saw it coming, but in the process of defending against the Twister, he opened himself up to the mount. I slipped on top and began setting up an arm triangle. Just as I was locking it in, he bucked me off and I ended up with him in my guard. We were back to square one.

I had just done some serious work, and technically it should have been eight to nothing in my favor. The only problem was that in Abu Dhabi they don't start counting points for the first five minutes. So it was still zero to zero. I had this guy in my guard, the judges had just started counting points, and I was completely spent. I wanted to play my Rubber Guard, show all those in attendance what no-gi grappling was really about, but the guy was really strong. If I got him in a submission while on my back and he pulled out of it, I would just have wasted several minutes and much energy. I just wanted to beat him and go to Brazil, so I didn't take any chances. From full guard I went to half guard, swept him, passed his guard, and then set up for the Twister again. After some struggling, I caught him, let everyone see that I could end the fight, and then let him go. I knew I was ahead on points, so I didn't take his back and lock in a choke. I could have done it, but I was spent. All that truly mattered was I had gotten the win.

It was a good move, because the last match in the tournament was twenty minutes instead of ten. And instead of not counting points for the first five minutes, the judges didn't count them for the first ten. I wasn't half as confident as I had been against Ashton because I was totally out of gas. And my opponent, Alan Teo, had run through his first two opponents in no time at all. He looked as if he'd just woken up from a refreshing nap.

When the two of us hit the mats, he caught me in head and arm control, which meant that I couldn't secure either the over-hooks or under-hooks and was basically helpless to sweep him. As the minutes passed with him lying on top of me, I started thinking about my Rubber Guard and all the other techniques I had devised, and my confidence began to grow. His head was right by my ear, and I could hear from his breathing that he was nervous. He was lying on top of me, not trying for any submissions. Perhaps he was waiting for the ten-minute mark, I didn't know. All I knew was

that if he wasn't expending any energy, then neither was I.

By the time ten minutes had gone by, I felt so confident that I could take this guy that I whispered in his ear, "You ready to play?" A second later, I fought his control and secured the under-hook, and then I racked up some points by sweeping him with Old School. Eight minutes were left, and I decided not to do anything more. I was just going to hold him until time ran out. That is not the style that I normally play, but all I could think about was Brazil. I was so close I could smell it.

It was easy to control him for six or seven minutes, but then all that holding began to take its toll. I started to get really tired, and he started bucking and thrashing, trying to shake me. He caught me in what he thought was a guillotine choke, so I started making fake choking and gurgling sounds. He didn't have it, but I knew it wouldn't be all that difficult for him to sweep me from our current position and rack up some points of his own. So I let him think he was on the verge of choking me unconscious. And it worked. He kept squeezing on my neck, and I kept making the fake noises. It was the most boring match ever, but everyone in the audience was screaming. Some yelled, "Alan, get him, choke him." Others shouted, "Eddie, you've only got a minute, hold on, you're going to win!"

When time ran out, Teo was still trying for the choke. The referee separated us, and I hopped up smiling. I was going to Brazil. There was also a good chance that I would face the notorious Royler Gracie while there. I wasn't sure how to feel, ecstatic or terrified.

2003 Abu Dhabi World Championships

While Rickson was considered the best jiu-jitsu practitioner in the world-renowned Gracie family, his younger brother Royler was by far the most accomplished. He'd competed against all the top jiu-jitsu practitioners in the Mundials, the world jiu-jitsu gi championships, and walked away the winner. He'd also won the Abu Dhabi Championships the three years he'd entered. In fact, he had been so dominant in Abu Dhabi nobody ever scored a point against him. His skills had been tested time and again, and he almost always stood in the winner's circle at the end of the night.

I wanted to fight him. I didn't care so much about winning the entire tournament. All I really cared about

was climbing onto the mat and defeating the infamous Royler Gracie. If I could do that, beat the man the whole world respected and feared, it would be bigger than winning the Abu Dhabi Championships five years in a row. And I didn't want to beat him just any old way—I wanted to beat him with the Twister. The move was illegal in the Abu Dhabi Championships, just as it had been illegal in the trials, but I didn't care. I was going to slap it on him and make him tap. Of course, I could get disqualified for performing the move and Royler would most likely go on to win the entire event, but the controversy would be huge. I would know, just as the world would know, that I had defeated him with my trademark move.

I began training harder than I ever had in my life; I even broke down and started lifting weights. Although my style wasn't strength dependent, I knew I needed all the leverage I could get. By game day, May 17, 2003, I felt strong, ready to take on the world. My nerves didn't kick in until I stepped into the Porra Arena in São Paulo, Brazil. With television cameras set up around the arena, broadcasting the action to grappling fans throughout Brazil, I knew right then that this was my ultimate test. I was about to compete in the biggest grappling tournament on the planet. Would I grab the bull by the horns and show everyone what my no-gi style was all about? Or, would I revert back to the scared competitor I had been several years before, too timid to do anything but hold his competitor in his half guard?

I learned the answer real fast when I stepped onto the mat with Jiu-Jitsu World Champion Gustavo Dantes in my first match of the night. Immediately I pulled half guard, swept him, and then set him up for the Twister. I knew I couldn't lock it in because then I would be disqualified before I faced Gracie, so as he began to defend against the Twister, I took his back and secured a rear naked choke. The easy victory made an impression on everyone in attendance, and when I went backstage a small crowd gathered around me. They were curious about my Rubber Guard, so I started giving them a demonstration. It turned into quite a little seminar. The only people who seemed disinterested were a couple of Brazilian jiu-jitsu players. I could tell by their sinister looks that they were thinking, "How does a brown belt know what works? He's an American, what does he know?"

I got so caught up in showing people how to perform the Rubber Guard that I lost track of time. Then all of a sudden the promoter was backstage

calling my name. I was up to fight Gracie. As if my body was working on autopilot, I stood up and headed out into the arena. When I reached the mat, everything seemed surreal. Across from me stood a fierce competitor I had seen on television and in magazines, a competitor I had always worshipped. I couldn't help but wonder what I was doing.

I stopped questioning what was going on the moment the referee signaled for us to begin our fight. As usual, I pulled half guard. That's not where he wanted to be, so he kept passing, trying for a better position. I knew that if he got whatever he was going for, my chances of winning would be a whole lot more difficult, so each time he passed my half guard, I pulled a move called the Jailbreak, which brought him back into my half guard. I don't think he had ever seen anything as unconventional as the Jailbreak before because he couldn't handle it. It went on like this for some time, Gracie passing my guard, and me pulling him back in with the Jailbreak. Eventually I realized that our little war wasn't doing either one of us any good, so I began searching for something. That's when I realized that I might be able to sweep him with this weird move that I had never done before. That threw me off. I found myself wondering if it was even possible to invent a move while grappling with Royler Gracie live on Brazilian TV in the Abu Dhabi World Championships.

Go for it, a voice in my head whispered, so I did. I wasn't sure if it was going to work, but then I saw him going over. I couldn't believe it. I didn't have much time to relish my ingenuity, however, because now I was stuck in Gracie's guard. He tried slapping on a triangle choke, but I broke free. I didn't like the feeling of being so close to my demise, so I quickly searched the arsenal of weapons I had stored in my mind and everything pointed toward sweeping him with a move called the 100 Percent (see Chapter 5). To execute the move, I backed out of his guard, baiting him. He raised up to grab my legs just as I'd hoped, and that's when I made my move. The goal of the move is to roll your opponent over so you can take his back, and the reason I called it the "100 Percent" is because if done correctly it should work 100 percent of the time. Well, I did it correctly, and the move didn't work. I had heard that Gracie's shoulders were double-jointed, but I never thought he would have been able to escape the 100 Percent.

After that little flurry, I was once again lying on my back with Gracie in my half guard. If I was going to win this, I decided, I was going to have to pull out the big guns, so I transitioned from half guard to full guard. I knew Gracie had grappled with hundreds of competitors through the years, but I doubted he had grappled with anyone who had trained so hard for no-gi competition. I threw my Rubber Guard at him to see how he handled it. My original intentions were to go for an Omoplata (see Chapter 2), but then I began thinking about his shoulder. If he was flexible enough to escape the 100 Percent, then he was most certainly flexible enough to escape an Omoplata. The next best option, I thought, was to go for a triangle choke.

While I scooted my legs up his body in hopes of securing the triangle, *bam*, he slid his knee through and passed my Rubber Guard. Instantly I went for Jailbreak, which he still hadn't caught on to. Instead of going back to half guard, however, I pulled Butterfly Guard, a position where both of your legs are inside your opponent's hips. I snatched the over-hook with my left arm, and as soon as I seized his wrist with my right hand, I thought, "Dude, you can set the triangle up from here. It would be perfect." Without thinking it through, I faked a sweep to the right side so that he would defend and open up his left side. Still controlling his wrist, I threw my leg over his head, secured a triangle choke, and cinched down.

Immediately Gracie tried to stand up to break my hold, so I over-hooked his left leg and sent him crashing back down on top of me. The only thing I worried about at that time was running out of time. I didn't want Gracie to be able to last until the bell, so to keep my hold from becoming un-cinched, I grabbed my left foot with both hands, something I had never done before. It was kind of a freak-out move on my part, but with Gracie now at my mercy, I didn't want to take any chances.

I squeezed my legs together as tightly as I could, thinking he was going to tap. But he didn't. He had probably been trapped in hundreds of triangles over the years, and he knew how to ride them out. I could hear Joe Rogan in the background, screaming at me to pull Gracie's head down. I didn't want to do that for fear he would escape, but eventually I just went for it. Only seconds after I pulled his head down, Gracie tapped his hand.

I jumped to my feet once the referee pulled us apart and strutted around the mat with my hands up in the air.

After making a few laps, I hugged Gracie to show my respect. When we pulled apart, it just hit me. That was all I had ever wanted to do—tap out Royler Gracie. I had wanted to defeat him by using the Twister, but now I knew this was far better. I had beaten him on the up-and-up. He had been training jiu-jitsu since he was two years old. I had been training less than ten years and was only a brown belt! It made those thousands upon thousands of hours I'd spent working on no-gi techniques worth it. From that point on, no one could claim that training without the gi didn't work because I had just proved that it did. I fell to my knees and started crying uncontrollably.

It wasn't until several minutes later that I realized I had two more matches to win in order to take the entire tournament. Even before I stepped back out onto the mat, I realized that such a feat was going to be hard to accomplish. What energy I had left after fighting Gracie had been blown on my racing emotions. I went out there and went through the motions, but in the end Leo Viera, who is a jiu-jitsu phenom just like Gracie, ended up winning on points. Though I didn't win the prize money, I returned to the

United States with something much more valuable.

The "Gi Versus No-Gi" Controversy

Back in 1993, Rorion Gracie created the first Ultimate Fighting Championship and forever changed the martial arts. After Rorion's brother Royce had choked a string of karate and kung fu practitioners unconscious in the first couple of events, millions of fight fans worldwide got to see that the Eastern fighting styles were not invincible, that in fact the ultimate self-defense discipline was grappling. Attendance levels in karate schools across the United States dropped, and those that kept their doors opened relied primarily on uninformed mothers signing their children up for classes. But once those children were old enough to search for the truth in fighting and self-defense on their own, most of them were steered toward some type of ground fighting. And it's all because of the Gracie family. If it weren't for them, I would probably be giving karate lessons rather than running a jiu-jitsu school that turns out some of the fiercest grapplers on the planet. In my opinion, the Gracies are the family of the millennium.

But no matter how much I owe them or how proud I am to have a black belt in Brazilian jiu-jitsu, I refuse to put on the blinders. Their system is flawed because they have stopped evolving it. They insist that in order to get good at grappling with no-gi, you first have to be a master grappling with the gi. But that just isn't true; my students are living proof. They only say that because that's what they teach. They specialize in the gi, so they are very fearful of people starting to train without it. It would be the same thing if you were a specialist at fixing Volkswagens. If people started buying Mercedes, even though it is a better car, you would try to convince them to drive Volkswagens because that is what you know how to fix. You might be okay at fixing Mercedes, but it is not your forte.

Fear of losing money is the only reason why black belt jiu-jitsu instructors keep perpetuating the lie that in order to get good without the gi you first have to get good at their style. I don't blame them because everyone's natural instinct is to want to be in control. And with the gi, they are utterly dominant. If you were to dress your average college wrestler up in a gi and have him grapple at any one of the Gracie schools, he is going to get tapped out ten times by everyone in the joint. But if you take the gi off him, those ten tap outs might get whittled down to just a few. So it changes things, and the jiu-jitsu instructors don't like the change.

In an attempt to prove the importance of training with the gi, traditional jiu-jitsu practitioners often cite history. They pull out the records from Abu Dhabi, the largest no-gi grappling tournament in the world, and explain how Brazilians who trained with the gi have won the majority of them. My answer is, "Of course they won!" Back in 1997 there were virtually no schools that trained without the gi. The no-gi game is new, and there are only a handful of competitors like myself breaking it down. A perfect example would be to pretend that Greco-Roman wrestling never existed, that the only form that involved takedowns and throws was judo, which utilizes a gi. Then, in 1997, a group of competitors decided to invent a style of judo that didn't involve the gi and call it Greco-Roman wrestling. Then they host their first no-gi competition and all the judo guys show up. Who do you think is going to win the first four or five events? All the judo guys. Now does that mean that if you want to win the Greco-Roman World Championships you have to train with a gi? No,

it just means there hasn't been any Greco-Roman wrestling before, and it will take a while for their style to evolve. And common sense will tell you that if you want to become effective at no-gi competition, you have to train without a gi.

I'm shocked that the argument is still going on. I know someone who had been training for eight or nine years with the gi. After doing a no-gi tournament he said to me, "I don't know what you are talking about, I did great and I owe it all to my gi training." I felt like slapping him and shouting, "It wasn't training with the gi that helped you, it was the grappling!" If he had spent eight or nine years training in a turtleneck sweater and spandex tights, he would have done just as well. So should everyone start wearing turtleneck sweaters and spandex?

It's not what you wear that makes you good; it is the actual grappling. Practitioners need to understand that. If they want to be a gi champion, become the meanest gi player alive, they should definitely train with the gi. But if all that matters is becoming a no-gi jiu-jitsu submission master, perhaps entering MMA competition, then they need to open their minds. Training jiu-jitsu with the gi is much better than training no jiu-jitsu at all. But why settle for something that is mediocre when there are a handful of guys out there, like me, willing to teach moves that are actually geared for no-gi grappling? If you go the traditional route, you'll develop bad habits that will haunt you once you get into the cage. You will waste much of your time learning stuff that never comes up in a no-gi competition. So if you allow someone to convince you that in order to get good at no-gi grappling you first have to learn how to fight with a gi, you've been brainwashed. You are going to learn basic balance, but you are not going to learn any true setups nor how to finish someone if you spend all your time holding on to the sleeve and collar.

Despite how earth-shatteringly obvious this seems to me, reality really hasn't sunken in with the majority of jiu-jitsu players. I tried to get the word out by traveling down to the birthplace of modern-day jiu-jitsu and tapping out Royler Gracie in the biggest no-gi tournament in the world, and still they give me no respect. It was the most historic match in Abu Dhabi history, the biggest upset. I didn't win by points; I forced Gracie to tap his hand in submission. But it all boils down to fear. They see what I have to offer coming over the horizon, and they don't

like it one bit. They took jiu-jitsu to a certain point, and now I'm taking it to a whole different level. Despite the verbal battles Royler Gracie and I have had, I respect what his family has done. I thank them for the arm bars, the triangles, and the rear naked choke off of the back, but I will never see the gi as a sacred piece of cloth. I see it as *the problem*.

10th Planet Jiu-Jitsu

A couple of years ago I came across the writings of a linguist and biblical scholar named Zecharia Sitchin who said that humans were created as slaves to mine gold for a superior humanlike race that lives on a 10th planet in our solar system. It was quite a theory to absorb, but it got me thinking. If there really was a race advanced enough to create humans for the sole purpose of mining gold, what else could they achieve? The Japanese had invented jiu-jitsu, and then the Brazilians made it better. But how crazy would ground fighting be on the 10th planet?

I like to think that it would resemble what I had come up with, full of positions like the Rubber Guard and Twister Side Control. It's not that I'm a revolutionary thinker; it's just that

I've always been open to the fact that jiu-jitsu isn't done. In order to improve something, you have to keep evolving it. You have to keep working on your setups and submissions, otherwise people will eventually begin to catch on. Unfortunately, the majority of jiu-jitsu instructors don't feel the same way. They look at me as if I'm from another planet, and that always brings a smile to my face. I might not have been born on the 10th planet, but I'd like to think that my style of jiu-jitsu certainly was.

Author Eddie Bravo (in white) in the Half Guard

1

...

The Half Guard

Introduction to the Half Guard

You can be an expert at climbing on top of your opponent and grabbing submissions from the mount. You can be a master at taking your opponent's back and slipping in a chokehold. But if you don't have a strong half guard, chances are you're not going to get into those positions as often as you'd like.

The half guard is the most important position in jiu-jitsu, the tree trunk of my system, because that's where the majority of fights take place. Most jiu-jitsu players prefer the full guard, but it's often quite difficult to trap your opponent between both of your legs. It's much easier to pull half guard and trap just one of your opponent's legs.

And most of the time your opponent will willingly fall into your half guard because they think it will cut down on their work—all they have to do is free their one leg, obtain side control or mount, and then finish with a submission. But it's not that easy, at least not with jiu-jitsu players who study my system. Instead of wasting all our energy just trying to maintain control of our opponent's leg, we lock it in place using the Lockdown. Instead of spending all our time on defense, we use double under-hooks to gain control of our opponent's upper body, which allows us to set up sweeps and submissions. By utilizing two simple techniques, we have turned a neutral position into an offensive one.

Key Concepts

- The half guard should be mastered first because whether you are a beginner or an advanced player, you will eventually find yourself on your back. Once there, trapping one of your opponent's legs between your legs in a half guard is much easier than trapping your opponent's entire body between your legs in a full guard.

- When your opponent has you trapped in an advantageous position, such as the mount or side mount, the half guard is always just one step away. By hooking one of your opponent's legs between your legs, you can regain control of the fight.

- By utilizing the Lockdown, under-hooks, and sweeps in the half guard, you can turn what most practitioners believe to be a neutral or weak position into an offensive one.

- Never look at the half guard as your opponent is half-passed your guard; look at it instead as you are halfway to getting a sweep or taking your opponent's back.

- No one sweep from half guard is the answer. Every opponent will move and react differently. The system of sweeps I describe is designed to react to this, moving from one sweep to the next so that you are always three steps ahead.

- Mastering the half guard allows you to be more aggressive in the mount and side mount because the fear of getting reversed and placed on your back is gone.

Lockdown

The Lockdown allows you to conserve energy, as well as disrupt your opponent's base and balance. In addition, the higher up on your opponent's leg that you secure the Lockdown, the more pressure you'll put on his calf muscle. With your opponent distracted by pain and trying to recover his balance, you can now focus on getting the double under-hooks.

To secure the Lockdown, I first bring my left leg over Joe's right leg.

I bring my right leg over the top of my left foot as I hook my right foot under Joe's right ankle.

I complete the Lockdown by stretching out, extending Joe's right leg and taking away the right side of his base.

Double Under-Hooks

The answer to turning the half guard into an offensive position is the double under-hooks. Once you have the double under-hooks and the Lockdown secure, you control your opponent's body. Sweeping your opponent and gaining a more favorable position, such as side mount or mount, is only one step away. It should be noted, however, that obtaining the double under-hooks is often quite a battle. The opponent on top needs at least one under-hook in order to pass your guard. If he tries passing without one, you can simply take his back. The key to winning the battle for the under-hooks while on the bottom is distracting your opponent by stretching him out in the Lockdown and continuing to pummel for position.

I start pummeling, getting my left arm under Joe's right arm on the same side as the Lockdown.

Using my right forearm, I control Joe's left arm as I reach through with my left arm.

3

I secure the double under-hooks.

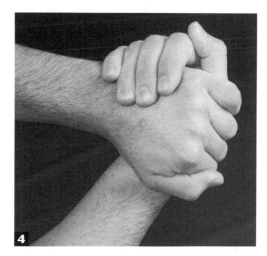

4

I grip my hands together, wrapping my fingers around the outside of my thumbs. This handclasp is known as the Gable Grip.

Half Guard Part 1: Sweeps

Old School

By securing both the Lockdown and the double under-hooks, you make it very difficult for an opponent to pass your half guard. But that doesn't necessarily mean you want to stay there. Although there are submissions you can go for in the half guard, there are a lot more submissions you can go for in both the side mount and mount. One way of getting to those superior positions is by utilizing a sweep. The first sweep that I invented, which I still find to be the most effective, is called Old School. I use it whenever possible because it's a very high percentage sweep that works on a wide range of opponents.

I've established the Lockdown position with double under-hooks, squeezing my hands tightly into the soft spot just below Joe's ribs and above his hip.

2 Keeping my left hook deep around Joe's waist, I release my grip, reaching under Joe's left foot with my right hand.

Circling out to my left, I release the Lockdown and get up to my right knee.

To complete the sweep, I use my under-hook to push forward and pull Joe's left leg out from underneath him, collapsing his base. Once Joe is swept, I make the transition into side control by back-stepping out with my right leg, making sure to keep my weight on Joe to avoid a scramble.

Plan B

Although Old School works a large percentage of the time, it can easily be countered. If your opponent over-hooks your left arm and throws all his weight into you by posting on his left leg, it makes it nearly impossible for you to get up to your knees and grab his foot. But just because you can't grab his foot doesn't mean you can't sweep him. With all his weight pressing into you, you can sweep him in the opposite direction using Plan B.

I've established the Lockdown with the double under-hooks.

Joe posts on his right leg and drives all his weight into me, making it impossible for me to get to my knees and grab his foot.

3 Feeling all of Joe's weight being placed on me, I fall back and put my right hand on the inside of Joe's left thigh. At the same time, I trap his right arm with my left arm to prevent him from posting out and potentially stopping the sweep.

4 Using the momentum of Joe's weight, I release the Lockdown and post with my right leg, pushing off the ground. As I do this, my right hand lifts Joe's left leg, rolling him over.

5 I complete the sweep by back-stepping out with my right leg into the side control position.

Twist Back

The Twist Back is a really good sweep to use if you can't get Old School and your opponent's base is just too low to be countered with Plan B. It's a great sweep because you don't have to release your under-hooks, and you're still using your opponent's weight to your advantage.

I've established the Lockdown with the double under-hooks.

2 I release the Lockdown and bring my left foot up to Joe's ankle.

I place my right leg under Joe's right leg, hooking under his knee.

Here I'm doing three things at once. With my right leg, I'm pushing up on Joe's knee. I use my left leg to pull his ankle down to the mat, and I use the double under-hooks to power him over.

5 As I sweep Joe over, I keep my right leg high, controlling Joe's right leg to prevent a last minute scramble.

Half and Half

The Half and Half is a hybrid sweep taken from Old School and Twist Back. This sweep is set up exactly like Old School except you are not grabbing your opponent's foot. Instead, you are using your weight and the power of the double under-hooks to tackle your opponent over. The double under-hooks, as with most sweeps, are the key elements to making this move a success.

I've established the Lockdown with the double under-hooks.

I post my right elbow on the ground so I can get to my knees.

3 Keeping my left hook deep around Joe's body, I base out on my right knee.

4 Circling out to my left, I stand up and quickly reestablish the double under-hook body lock.

5 To complete the sweep, I squeeze the body lock tight to pull Joe's waist toward mine, while at the same time I drive my upper body into his. Joe loses his balance and topples over, allowing me to move directly into side control.

Half and Twist

If any one move worked 100 percent of the time, you wouldn't have to learn anything else. Unfortunately, no such move exists, so every jiu-jitsu player needs as many moves as possible to get to their desired goal. Although the Half and Half is a good sweep, it can be countered. If you are able to base out on your right knee but your opponent counters by balancing and pushing his weight down on you, the Half and Twist is the perfect sweep.

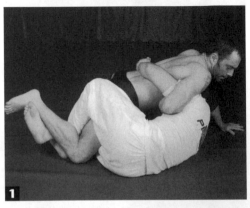

Once again, I've established the Lockdown with double under-hooks.

I post on my right arm. As I attempt to get to my knees, I keep my left under-hook nice and deep around Joe's body.

Once I've based out on my knee and re-established a tight body lock, I'm back in Half and Half, attempting to tackle Joe to the mat.

As Joe fights the Half and Half by balancing and pushing his weight back into me, I sneak my right foot to the outside of Joe's right knee.

I push on the outside of Joe's knee with my right foot and pull on his right ankle with my left leg. With each of my legs moving in an opposite direction, it creates a scissorslike motion. At the same time, I fall toward my back and use the double under-hooks to power Joe over the top of me.

6 To keep Joe from scrambling away before I can transition to side control, I maintain control of his right leg by holding my right leg high.

Half Quarterback Sweep

This is a move that does not necessarily take place in your half guard. It takes place in a position I call the "quarter guard," which is where your opponent is able to free his leg from the Lockdown and almost pass your half guard—except you are able to catch his foot with your knees. A lot of jiu-jitsu players give up in this position and let their opponent pass, but that doesn't have to be the case. As long as you can hold on to your opponent's foot and maintain the double under-

hooks, you still have the power to sweep your opponent.

Joe was able to free his leg from the Lockdown and almost passed my guard, but I was able to trap his foot with my knees in the quarter guard.

2 I release the body lock from around Joe, using my right arm to get to my knees.

3

Once on my knees I quickly reestablish a tight body lock around Joe's waist.

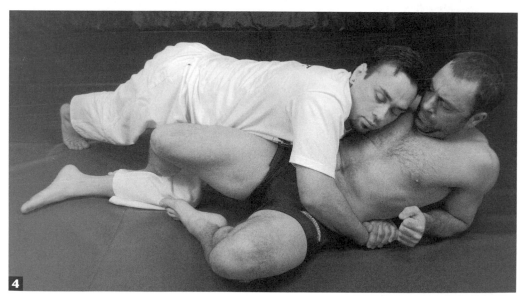

4

Using the power of the body lock, I squeeze my arms in toward my waist while at the same time pressing into Joe with my head and shoulders, folding him over just as in Half and Half.

Quarter Twist Back

The Quarter Twist Back is another option from the quarter guard. When your opponent presses his weight down on you, making it difficult to get up to your knees, you can use his weight against him by employing this move. It is very similar to the Twist Back because you're twisting your opponent's knee to help pull him over. As I mentioned before, it's important not to give up when your opponent is almost past your half guard. As long as you can trap his foot with your knees and hold on to the double under-hooks, there's always an option.

Once again Joe was able to free his leg from the Lockdown and almost passed my guard, but I was again able to catch his foot with my knees in the quarter guard.

While Joe presses the majority of his weight down into me, not allowing me to get to my knees, I maneuver my left leg up to Joe's right ankle.

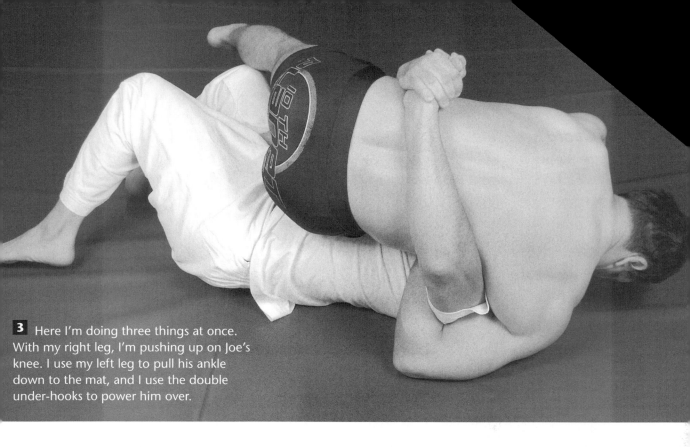

3 Here I'm doing three things at once. With my right leg, I'm pushing up on Joe's knee. I use my left leg to pull his ankle down to the mat, and I use the double under-hooks to power him over.

4

Once I have Joe rolled over, I move up to establish side control.

Sweep

Some Jiu-Jitsu players like to stay close to their opponents' bodies when they attempt to pass the guard, while others like to stand up and dance around. When dealing with the latter, it is important that you find some way to close the distance and force your opponent to commit so you can either land a submission or go for a sweep. This can often be a daunting task, especially with an opponent who stays on the outside and avoids your legs. The X-Guard Sweep, however, is the perfect strategy to use in this situation. Once you have executed the first couple of moves, your opponent has only two options—get swept over to his back or drop down to his knees to counter the move. If he counters by dropping to his knees, the move has still been a success. You are now in a perfect position to pull your opponent into your half guard and begin setting up one of the other submissions or sweeps described in this chapter.

1 Joe hovers above me, waiting for the perfect opportunity to sneak through my guard.

2

After scooting between Joe's legs, I place my left leg on Joe's right leg and under-hook his left leg with my right arm. This gives me control of his lower body.

3

I grab the outside of Joe's right ankle with my left hand, making it so Joe can't counter by walking forward. At the same time, I sneak my right leg up and place it on the right side of his crotch.

4 To bring Joe down, I have to do three things at once. I pull on Joe's right ankle with my left hand, pull on his left leg with my right under-hook, and extend my legs. Once Joe is down, I come up to establish side control.

Double X

The Double X is another move that can be employed against an opponent who is trying to pass your guard in the standing position. Your opponent can counter the move, just as in the X-Guard Sweep, by dropping down to his knees. But then you will be in a much better position to pull him into your half guard and begin setting up one of the other sweeps or submissions described here.

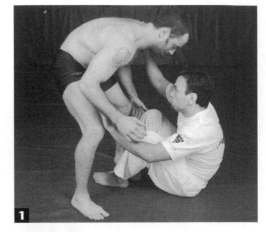

Joe hovers above me, waiting for the perfect opportunity to sneak through my guard.

After scooting between Joe's legs, I place my left leg on Joe's right leg and under-hook his left leg with my right arm. This gives me control of his lower body.

I bring up my right instep and place it on Joe's right thigh. At the same time, I grab the outside of his right ankle with my left hand.

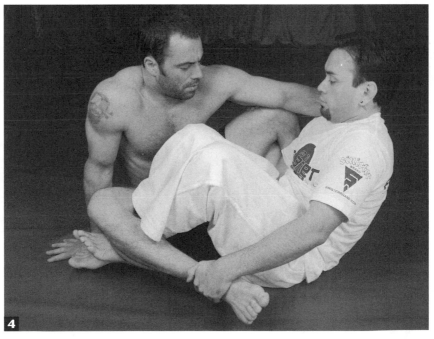

Now I drive out, pushing with my legs while pulling with my arms, sending Joe to the mat. Once Joe is down, I come up to establish the side control position.

Half Guard Part 3: Submissions

Apollo (with Sweep)

Submissions from the half guard are rare, but they do present themselves from time to time. One such submission is the Apollo Arm Triangle. When you cinch down on the Lockdown, your opponent will occasionally get distracted and look back to see why his leg is in pain. If you have your opponent's right leg in the Lockdown, he will look over his right shoulder. As he does this, his left arm will come up toward your head, leaving it extremely vulnerable. That's when you should trap it and go for the Apollo Arm Tri-

angle. Sometimes, however, you can't get your opponent to tap. Arm triangles work the best when you are on top because you can use your weight to assist you. If this is the case, you can still use your positioning to set up the sweep.

I've got Joe in the Lockdown with an under-hook on his right side.

I trap Joe's left arm by making an S-grip behind my head.

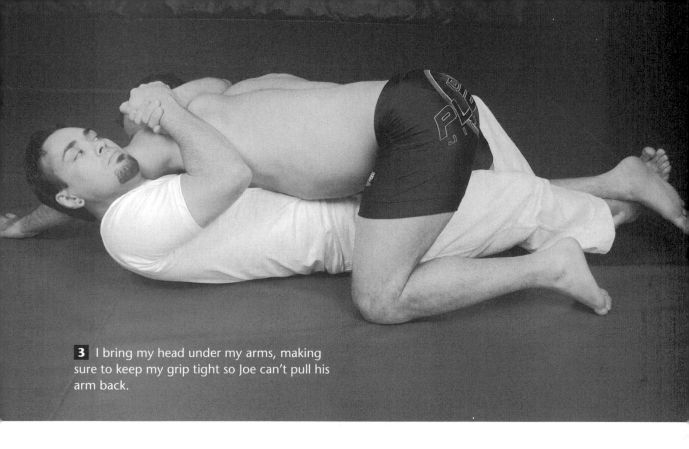

3 I bring my head under my arms, making sure to keep my grip tight so Joe can't pull his arm back.

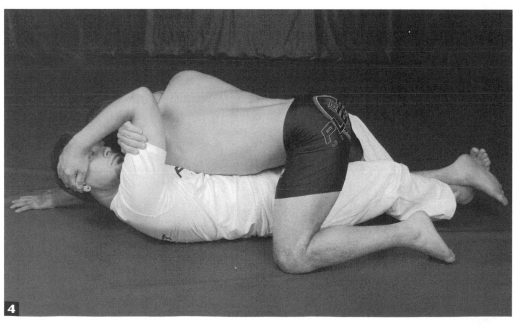

4

I move into the arm triangle by putting my left hand on my right bicep and my right hand on my right ear, squeezing.

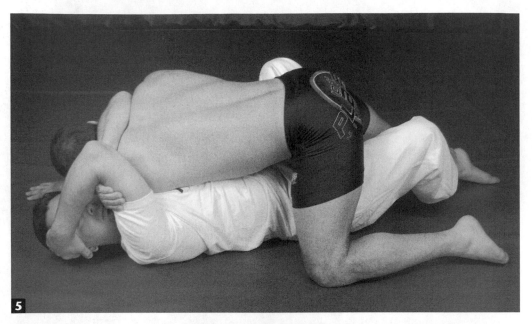

I squeeze the arm triangle, but Joe refuses to tap. Knowing I need to sweep Joe to the right, I work to get my left foot to the inside of Joe's right hip, which is known as a Butterfly Hook.

Posting my right leg on the mat, I drive up with my left leg. Because Joe's left arm is trapped in the arm triangle, he can't place it on the mat and stop the sweep.

7

Once on top, I continue to squeeze my arms, only now I'm using my weight to add pressure, forcing Joe to tap in submission.

Kamikaze Calf Crank

This is a sly submission from the half guard that you can apply without the use of your hands. After I discovered it, I used it all the time in the gym to get my opponents to tap. It worked so well I decided to start using it in competition, but I didn't have the same type of success. I soon realized the reason why. In competition, my opponents were all hopped up on adrena- line, which meant that they were more tolerant to pain. Because of that, I usu- ally go for the higher percentage sub- missions first. If they don't work, I'll try for the Kamikaze Calf Crank. The worst possible outcome is that you make your opponent very uncomfort- able, and while he is trying to escape the hold, you can work on setting up either a sweep or another submission.

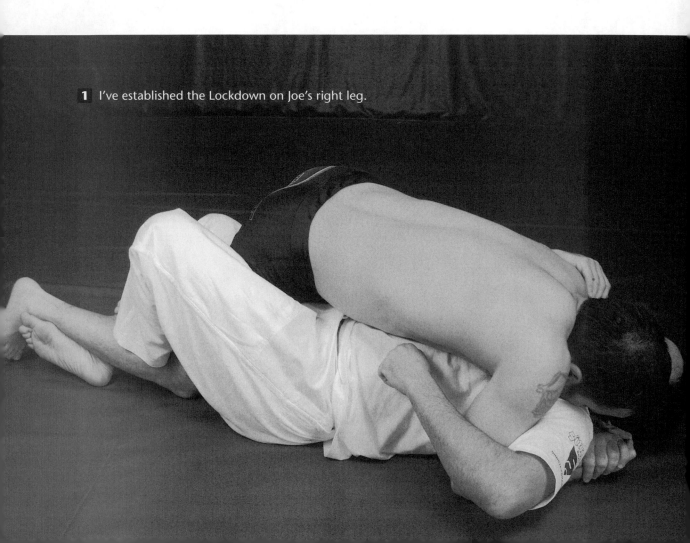

1 I've established the Lockdown on Joe's right leg.

Releasing the Lockdown, I move my right foot over Joe's right leg.

3

I use my right leg to push out while curling my left leg into my body, putting extreme pressure on Joe's calf.

Ken Shamrock Toehold

This is one of the first submissions I learned from the half guard, and it works really well on opponents who like to post their legs high up near your head. If you are able to grab a foot, the submission is pretty much yours. Getting your opponent to tap, however, can often be difficult, especially in tournaments where your opponent's pain tolerance is increased due to an adrenaline rush. Nevertheless, it is a good move to learn because when you're down in the dumps and

nothing else is working, you can still pull this one off.

Here again, I've established the Lockdown with the double under-hooks.

I slip under Joe's left arm and grip the top of his left foot with my right hand.

3

I reach around Joe's leg with my left arm and grip my right wrist.

4

Rolling to the left takes away Joe's base and puts him on his back. To secure the hold, I push his foot down toward the mat with my right hand while pulling his ankle toward my head with my left arm.

Electric Chair with Sweep

The Electric Chair is another submission that should be utilized when your opponent posts his outside leg high up near your head. If you can get an under-hook around his leg and then stretch him out with the Lockdown, you take away his base. Then it's only a matter of turning your opponent belly-down so you can stretch him out even further and put an enormous amount of pressure on his legs. Some guys have the flexibility to take the pressure, in which case you just follow through with a sweep.

As I secure the Lockdown with double under-hooks, Joe posts with his right leg and presses his weight down into me.

I release the body lock and scoop up Joe's left leg with a deep right under-hook.

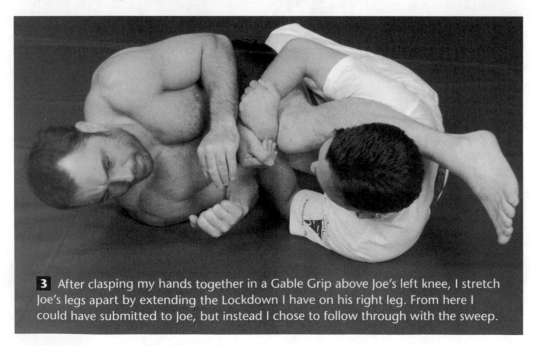

3 After clasping my hands together in a Gable Grip above Joe's left knee, I stretch Joe's legs apart by extending the Lockdown I have on his right leg. From here I could have submitted to Joe, but instead I chose to follow through with the sweep.

Keeping Joe's right leg secured in the Lockdown, I roll my weight forward and put Joe on his back. I then secure his head and arm by clasping my hands together in a Gable Grip as I make my transition into side control (below).

Demonstration of Rubber Guard

2

❖❖❖

Rubber Guard

Introduction to the Full Guard

When I first started training jiu-jitsu, I avoided the full guard like the plague. I thought my legs were too short to capture an opponent between my legs and land submissions, so I spent all my time learning how to sweep an opponent from half guard. I became so good at it that I began to believe the half guard was the answer to fighting from your back. Then a muscle-bound guy who had never before trained jiu-jitsu came to practice. I thought I was going to destroy him from my half guard, but I couldn't do anything. It was his first day training jiu-jitsu ever, and I could not catch him in one single submission. After twenty minutes of grappling, I climbed off the mat and hung my head in shame.

I thought the guy had to be some sort of phenom. But then five minutes later I saw a good friend of mine, who is my exact size and had been grappling an equal amount of time, absolutely destroy the same guy in his guard. In just a couple of minutes, my friend had made the brute tap seven times with triangle chokes and arm bars. I knew right then that I would never be a complete fighter until I learned how to fight from the guard. So the very next day, I had my friend show me the basics, starting with the arm bar.

Up until that point, I was simply holding on to my opponent's arm and going for the submission. Although such a tactic worked with beginners, advanced players would see the submission coming and pull their arms free. I thought there was nothing I could do to prevent that from happening, but then I learned that if I placed my leg over my opponent's shoulder, locking it in place, I eliminated his ability to pull his arm free. Once I became good at that technique, I started landing arm bars all the time from the guard. I fell in love with the position, just as I had fallen in love with the half guard.

But then I ran into some problems. When I tried locking the shoulder and going for the arm bar on bigger and stronger opponents, instead of trying to pull their arms free, they pressed all their weight down into me, making it nearly impossible for me to extend their arms and lock in the submission. Unable to find a solution on my own, I went to my instructor Jean Jacques Machado and asked him what to do. He told me that with larger opponents I shouldn't be attempting to lock out their arms from my back. Instead, I should lock their shoulders and then sweep them instead of trying to finish them. Once they are on their backs, they can't use their weight against me and the arm bar is much easier.

It worked so well on the bigger opponents, I started using the technique on everyone. I became so confident in the guard that every time I watched the Ultimate Fighting Championship (UFC) and one of my fellow jiu-jitsu players secured his opponent in his guard, I would get excited. My

friends watching with me didn't know anything about jiu-jitsu, and I would shout, "This guy is going to win, he knows jiu-jitsu. A submission is coming any second now; he's got him in his guard!"

Ten minutes later, the jiu-jitsu player was still on his back, not doing anything. After the exact same thing happened with a number of world jiu-jitsu champions whom the UFC had brought aboard hoping that they would become the next Royce Gracies, I began to wonder what the heck was going on. I was just a blue belt at the time, yet in the gym I was sweeping and setting up submissions on my opponents all the time from the guard.

Over the course of several UFC events, I began to get more and more embarrassed. I raved about jiu-jitsu to everyone, bragging how it was the ultimate martial art, but at the same time the jiu-jitsu players entering mixed martial arts (MMA) competitions were consistently losing. That's when I asked myself, "What could possibly be the difference between training in the gym and entering MMA competition?" Immediately the answer came. It was the gi. When executing the guard, 99.9 percent of jiu-jitsu players have become accustomed to controlling their opponent's body by holding on to the sleeve and collar. They fake a collar choke to set up for the arm bar or they fake the collar choke to set up the triangle. If you take away their opponent's collar, they have no setups to transition into the submission. Then they just lie there on their backs like a fish out of water.

It became evident that what had worked for Gracie back when no one knew anything about submissions wasn't going to work in this day and age, not with virtually all MMA competitors wise to submission defense. If they wanted to start getting finishing holds again, they would have to start training without the gi. They needed to develop setups that weren't based on the collar and the sleeve because setups are everything in fighting. Every wrestler knows how to execute a single- and double-leg takedown. Every boxer knows how to throw a jab and a cross. But what allows them to be successful with those techniques is how well they set them up. If a jiu-jitsu player bases all his setups while in the guard off the collar and sleeve, and then he enters an MMA competition where competitors don't wear a gi, he is lost.

I didn't want to have to relearn jiu-jitsu or break a bunch of bad habits.

I wanted to learn a form of jiu-jitsu that was MMA- and street-ready, so I started changing my guard back in 1996. Instead of grabbing my opponent's collar and sleeve, I started holding on to my opponent using over-hooks, under-hooks, and head control. Instead of setting up submissions by faking a collar choke, I set up submissions by faking with a sweep. I tried everything I could think of, and while most of my inventions fell by the wayside, I kept dozens of others. In the matter of just a few years, I had developed a guard system that was just as effective as the traditional guard for defense, but it was also extremely effective at offense. It is based on just a few basic positions, the most important of which is Mission Control.

Rubber Guard

Once you master Mission Control (see page 65), you'll move on to other guard positions described in this book such as the New York and Invisible Collar. Although many of these positions and techniques require flexibility, if you practice them long enough, eventually your knees and hips will feel as though they are made from rubber. Hence the name of my guard system—the Rubber Guard.

Key Concepts

- If you train jiu-jitsu with a gi and then enter a no-gi tournament, you've just lost all your handles and setups that utilize the collar and sleeve. Therefore, you must learn how to control your opponent using the over-hooks, under-hooks, and head control.

- Hip movement and hip control is the most important element in jiu-jitsu. You can use your hips and legs to control your opponent and keep him off balance, forcing him to focus on regaining his base rather than passing your guard.

- It's easy to lose control of a fight if you don't know how to relax while fighting from your back. The only way to get comfortable fighting from your back is to drill and practice from there as much as possible.

- Having a tight guard game eliminates your fear of going to your back, which gives you more confidence when attempting submissions from the top.

- Utilizing setups from the guard are key to finishing your opponent. Use the positions given to you in this chapter to help set up submissions.

- Always move while in your guard to keep your opponent guessing. Just lying still and holding on will never get you anywhere.

- It takes time and a lot of practice to get the flexibility needed to play the Rubber Guard. Don't get discouraged and give up. Have patience and drill as much as possible so you feel comfortable working from these positions.

Mission Control

Utilizing the Mission Control position allows you to be both offensive and defensive from the guard. Locking your leg high up on your opponent's back keeps your opponent's posture broken down, guards you from punches, and frees up an arm that can be used to hunt for submissions.

Laurence postures up in my guard.

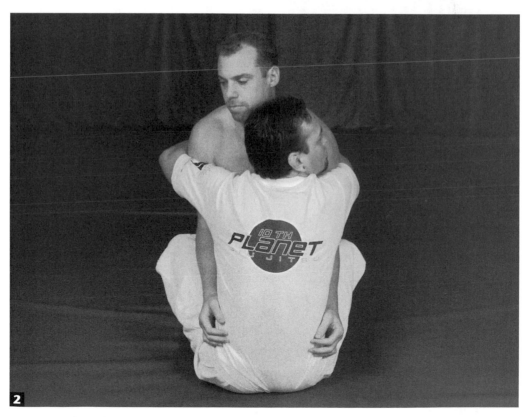

In order to be offensive, I need to break Laurence down into my guard. I unlock my legs into the open guard so I can come up and wrap my arms around Laurence's body.

I pull Laurence down into my guard by falling back, keeping my grip nice and tight.

To keep Laurence from posturing back up, I immediately bring my left leg up, place my ankle on the back of his neck, hook my right wrist under my ankle, and then lock my hands together by forming a Gable Grip with my right palm facing down. Now I've got Laurence in Mission Control.

Rubber Guard Part 1: Mission Control

Over-Hook Triangle from Mission Control

Once you've established Mission Control, you'll probably find that most of your opponents choose to keep their hands on your chest for defense. In order to be offensive from the guard, however, you need to bring one of your opponent's hands down to the mat. This can be hard to achieve while playing the traditional guard because you're using all four limbs to control your opponent, but that isn't the case with the Rubber Guard. You can use your free hand to force one of your opponent's hands down to the mat, and then keep it there by over-hooking your opponent's arm. With your opponent's arm isolated, numerous submission opportunities open up, including the triangle choke.

I've broken Laurence down into Mission Control.

If I want to be offensive, I need to get Laurence's hand to the mat. I can achieve this by reaching under his right arm with my left arm, punching it through. While I do this, I maintain Mission Control by holding my ankle in place with my right wrist.

Once I have broken Laurence's grip, forcing his right hand to the mat, I quickly secure a tight over-hook on his right arm to keep him from putting his hand back on my chest.

Now that I have a tight over-hook on Laurence's right arm, I let go of my leg and use my right hand to grab Laurence's wrist.

I push Laurence's arm back, throwing my leg over his left arm and wrapping it across the back of his neck.

5

6

I make a figure four with my legs by throwing my left leg over my right, and I clasp my hands together using a Gable Grip behind Laurence's head. I lock in the choke as I squeeze my knees together and pull down on his head.

Over-Hook Omoplata from Mission Control

Anytime you are able to get your opponent's hand to the mat, you've got an opportunity to execute an Omoplata.

I've broken Laurence down into Mission Control.

I work to get Laurence's hand to the mat by reaching under his right arm with my left arm.

Now that I've broken Laurence's grip and forced his right hand to the mat, I quickly secure a tight over-hook on his right arm to keep him from putting his hand back on my chest.

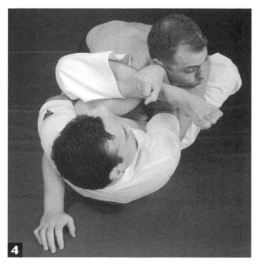

4

I use my right hand to bring my left leg down in front of Laurence's face.

5

Pushing off Laurence's hip with my right foot swivels my body slightly in a clockwise motion. While I spin, I bring my left leg over his shoulder to isolate his right arm between my legs. To secure the hold on his arm, I place my right leg over my left.

6

Bringing my right leg back for base, I reach around Laurence's body and pull myself forward, putting tremendous pressure on Laurence's right shoulder and forcing him to tap.

The Duda

It can be quite a battle trying to get your opponent's hand down to the mat because most jiu-jitsu players know they'd be opening themselves up for a number of submissions. If you have a larger or stronger opponent in your guard and you just can't get his hand down to the mat, the Duda is the perfect submission.

Once again, I've broken Laurence down into Mission Control.

Laurence keeps his arms gripped tightly together, making it difficult for me to punch my arm through. Instead of fighting him, I reach around his right arm and grab his wrist.

Pushing off of Laurence's hip with my right leg, my body swivels in a clockwise motion. As I turn, I bring my right leg around to the left side of Laurence's head. As I place my right leg over my left, I also clasp my hands together using the Gable Grip with my right palm down. To complete the submission, I thrust my hips and pull my left arm in using my right hand, crushing Laurence's wrist.

Rubber Guard Part 2:
New York

New York

After you've broken your opponent down in Mission Control and wrestled his hand to the mat, you can keep it there by using the New York. Once you've got a good feel for this position, numerous submission opportunities become available.

Here I again have broken Laurence down into Mission Control.

I reach around Laurence's right arm with my left hand, punching it through and breaking his grip.

Once I have broken Laurence's grip, I reach around my knee with my left arm, pinning Laurence's right arm to the mat. Just as in Mission Control, my right foot remains on Laurence's left hip.

Triangle Choke from New York

Triangles from the guard have proven to be extremely successful in both MMA and jiu-jitsu competitions. Here is an effective way of setting up the triangle choke from the New York position.

I've established the New York, successfully pinning Laurence's right hand to the mat.

I grab Laurence's left hand with my right hand and push it through my legs.

I throw my right leg over Laurence's left shoulder.

To secure the triangle, I throw my left leg over my right leg and squeeze my knees together. Then I clasp my hands together behind Laurence's head, using a Gable Grip, and pull his head down.

Jiu-Jitsu Unleashed

Left Arm Bar from New York

Once you've locked your opponent's right arm to the mat with the New York, a lot of times your opponent will reach across with his left arm in an attempt to free his captured arm. When he does this, all you have to do to get the arm bar is trap your opponent's shoulder, grab his left arm, and thrust your hips. If you execute the move properly and with speed, your opponent won't see it coming.

I've established the New York, successfully trapping Laurence's hand to the mat.

As Laurence moves his left arm across my body in an attempt to free his right arm, I push my right leg off his hip and trap his shoulder with my right leg.

I place my right leg over my left, and then grab Laurence's left arm while thrusting with my hips, securing the arm bar.

Omoplata from New York

When your opponent is in your guard and you've locked his hand to the mat, the Omoplata is never far away. If you have trouble locking it in and getting your opponent to tap, don't be too hasty to abandon the move. The Omoplata can also be used as a control position by controlling your opponent's arms with your legs. Depending on how your opponent reacts, you can usually transition from the Omoplata submission attempt into a number of other finishing holds, as you will see in the following pages. If no such finishing holds present themselves, at the very least you can use the Omoplata to sweep your opponent, putting you into side control.

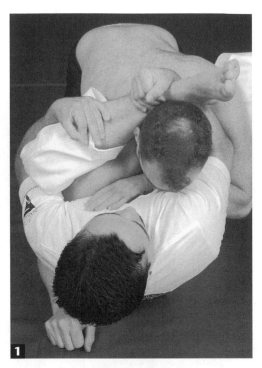

Again, I've established the New York, successfully pinning Laurence's hand to the mat.

I push off Laurence's head with my right forearm, creating enough distance to bring my leg over to the right side of his head.

I push off Laurence's hip with my right leg. At the same time, I also push my left leg across the front of Laurence's face.

Once I'm able to sit out, I quickly trap Laurence's arm by throwing my right leg over my left leg in the figure four position. To ensure Laurence doesn't tuck his head and roll out of the submission, I control his legs with my left arm.

Bringing my right leg back for base, I reach around Laurence's body with both hands. To finish the submission, I sit up and press my hips forward. With a tremendous amount of pressure being placed on Laurence's right shoulder, he is forced to tap.

Omoplata to Inverted Arm Bar

As I previously mentioned, there are many submissions that you can transition into from the Omoplata. Once you have sat out and trapped your opponent's shoulder, you've established the Omoplata control position. From here, sometimes your opponent's arm gets in the way and stops you from sitting up and securing the shoulder lock. When this happens, there's no need to get discouraged. The inverted arm bar is right there for the taking.

In this sequence, I've established the Omoplata control position on Laurence.

Capitalizing on Laurence's isolated arm, I grab his wrist with both hands and force it up, hyperextending his arm.

Omoplata to Straight Arm Bar

In this sequence I've presented another option in capturing the inverted arm bar, only here you reconfigure your legs so that when your opponent rolls through, countering the inverted arm bar, you can move directly into the straight arm bar.

I was able to establish the Omoplata control position on Laurence by sitting out and trapping his shoulder.

While maintaining control of Laurence's legs using my left arm, I reconfigure my legs by placing my right leg over Laurence's shoulder.

As I grab Laurence's wrist with both hands and press up, he feels the pressure being placed on his arm and rolls in an attempt to break the lock.

Keeping control of Laurence's arm as he rolls, I push with my right leg so that it slides across his torso. I also bring my left leg down to his head.

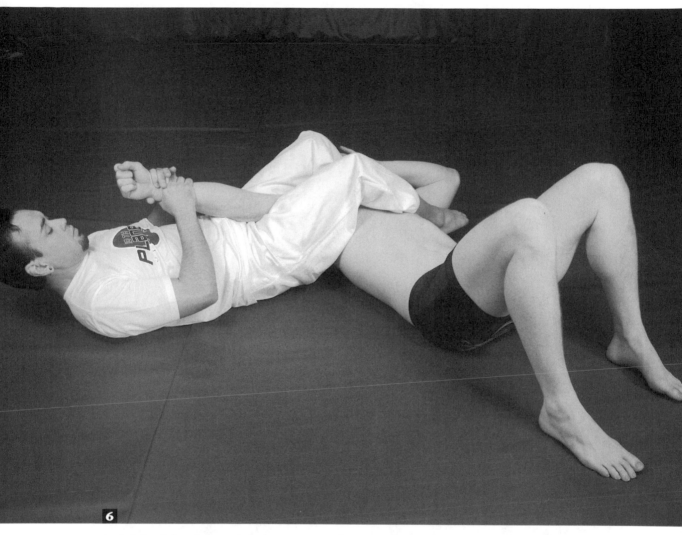

As I sit back for the arm bar, I squeeze my legs together and elevate my hips, hyper-extending Laurence's arm.

Omoplata to Triangle

The reason why you place your right leg over the top of your left leg in the Omoplata control position is to lock your opponent's shoulder, giving you control of his upper body. But quite often your opponent will posture up, breaking the lock your legs have on his shoulder. Ideally you don't ever want to lose control of your opponent's upper body, but in some situations it can be difficult to get your right leg on top of your left leg to keep your opponent down. If you can feel your oppo-

nent break the lock and time when he will posture up, you can spin back to the triangle choke.

I've secured the Omoplata control position on Laurence's right shoulder.

Laurence breaks the shoulder lock by posturing up.

Timing his reaction, I spin in a counterclockwise direction. As I do this, I hook my right leg around Laurence's head to set up the triangle choke.

Placing my right leg underneath my left knee, I squeeze my legs together. At the same time, I clasp my hands using a Gable Grip and pull his head toward my body.

The Go-Go Plata

I stole this move from jiu-jitsu phenom Nino Schembri because it wasn't hard for me to see just how often it presented itself during the transition to the Omoplata. It is a tricky move that requires a lot of flexibility, but it is extremely effective.

I've established the New York, successfully pinning Laurence's hand to the mat.

Just as if I were setting up the Omoplata, I bring my left leg in front of Laurence's face.

I force my left foot up with my right hand, making sure that I have my foot under Laurence's neck.

I push my heel up with my right hand as I reach around Laurence's head with my left hand, grabbing my foot. From here I twist my foot in a counterclockwise motion, cranking Laurence's neck and choking him at the same time.

Invisible Collar

Once you are able to break your opponent down using Mission Control and secure his hand to the mat using New York, the Omoplata is readily available. Most players know this and will not allow you to pull your right leg out to secure the Omoplata. You can still bring your left leg over your opponent's head, but without pulling your right leg out and putting it on top of your left ankle, you can't complete the Omoplata. In answer to this problem, I devised the Invisible Collar. It doesn't always work—some opponents can take the pain, while others can't. It actually tends to work better on larger opponents because they have less room to maneuver. But regardless of your opponent's size, you should be able to inflict enough pain to at least force your opponent to free your right leg, giving you the Omoplata. If you still can't secure the Omoplata for whatever reason, the Invisible Collar also presents other submission possibilities and transitions.

I've established the New York, successfully pinning Laurence's right hand to the mat.

I start the Omoplata by pushing my forearm against the right side of Laurence's neck to create separation. Laurence, sensing the Omoplata setup, uses his left arm to pin my right leg.

Knowing the Omoplata is out of reach, I transition to the Invisible Collar. I achieve this by hooking my left leg with my right wrist and pulling down.

To finish the Invisible Collar, I bring my right foot up and hook it on top of my left. Then I bend my right elbow and drive it down on Laurence's right collarbone, using my legs to assist.

If Laurence withstands the pain and doesn't tap, I have another option. Because I have his right arm isolated, I transition to the inverted arm bar by pushing his arm back against my leg, hyperextending his arm.

Rubber Guard Part 3: Spider Web

Basic Arm Bar to Spider Web

When I first started training jiu-jitsu, every time I went for an arm bar from the guard my opponent would press his weight down into me, making it nearly impossible for me to extend my hips and lock in the submission. This was a big setback because arm bars are the most common submission from the guard. I asked Jean Jacques what to do, and he told me that when grappling with a larger or stronger opponent I shouldn't attempt to lock out his arm while lying on my back. Instead, I should use the control I had on my opponent's arm to sweep him. Once I placed him on his back, he could no longer press his weight down into me and the arm bar would come much easier. I tried it out on my larger opponents and it worked so well that I started using the strategy on everyone. I named the position Spider Web because once I had my opponent on his back, he was little more than a fly caught in my web. He might still be alive and kicking, but it was only a matter of time before I crawled down the web and finished the fly off. The success I had with this position helped

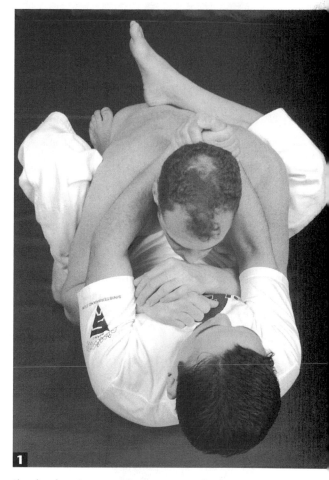

I've broken Laurence's posture and brought him into my guard.

me realize just how important it was not to simply jump into a submission all at once. If I had continued jumping into the arm bar from the guard and hoping for the best, I never would have realized that there was another option available.

I elevate my hips up into Laurence's right armpit and cross my feet. This locks Laurence's shoulder and eliminates the possibility of him pulling his arm free.

I hook my left arm over Laurence's right arm and reach my hand all the way over to my left hip. Then I hook Laurence's left leg with my right hand.

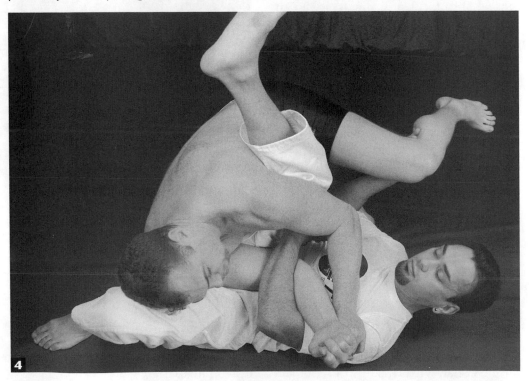

Keeping my left hook tight so Laurence can't pull his arm free, I use my right hook around Laurence's leg to help spin my hips in a counterclockwise motion. As I spin, Laurence's body gets pushed to his right. Because I still have control of his right arm, he cannot post his hand on the mat to stop the sweep.

As Laurence gets swept to his back, I keep my legs tight against his body and cross my feet. With my left arm still hooked around Laurence's right arm, I have the option of leaning back and pulling on my left arm to break Laurence's handgrip. If I were able to achieve this, I could fall back and arch my hips, securing an arm bar. But I feel this option is too risky. Laurence is expecting the arm bar, and if he scrambles up to his knees he can force me back into my guard. To keep him from achieving his goal of getting to his knees, I immediately reach back after the sweep with my right arm and hook Laurence's right leg. I'm now in the Spider Web position and can work on breaking Laurence's grip.

Arm Crush to Arm Bar

The Arm Crush is a great submission because you can execute it without the use of your arms, thereby maintaining control of your opponent while working for a submission. But there *are* a couple of catches. The first catch is that the Arm Crush is a pain move, and if your opponent has a high pain tolerance, sometimes it's difficult to get him to tap. The second catch is that the hold will sometimes slip if there is a lot of sweat. In either case, you can still transition into the arm bar.

I'm ready to attack now that I've swept Laurence into the Spider Web position.

Jiu-Jitsu Unleashed

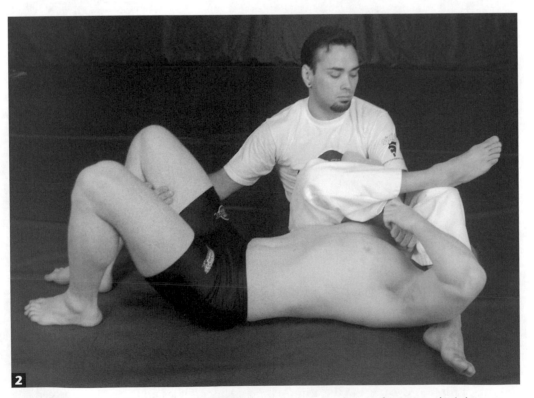

Uncrossing my feet, I bring my right leg over and place it on top of Laurence's right arm, which is bent.

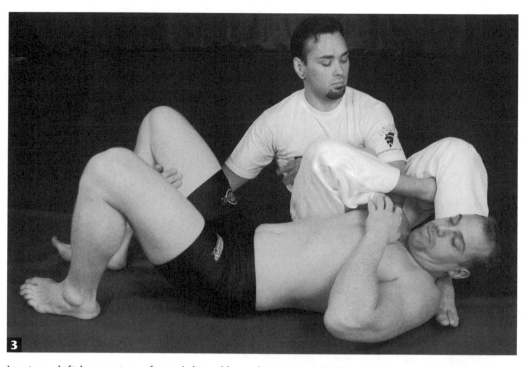

3

I put my left leg on top of my right ankle and secure my left foot underneath Laurence's head. With my left arm still wrapped under Laurence's right arm, I can use it as a fulcrum while applying downward pressure with my legs.

If the hold slips due to the sweat or Laurence refuses to tap from the pain, I can still go for the straight arm bar. I achieve this by placing my left foot on the other side of Laurence's head, squeezing my knees together, and elevating my hips as I fall back. It is important to notice that I've maintained control of Laurence's legs this whole time by keeping my right arm hooked around his right leg.

4

Triangle Arm Bar

It's important to master a few techniques that you can use to trap your
opponent from the Spider Web. The
arm crush is the first option, but your
opponent can stop you from bringing
your leg over by simply raising up his
arms. If this should happen, you can
do what I do and immediately transition into the Triangle Arm Bar. The
submission is just as high on my list as
the Arm Crush because you don't have
to let go of your opponent's right leg
to pull it off.

I'm ready to attack now that I've swept
Laurence into the Spider Web position.

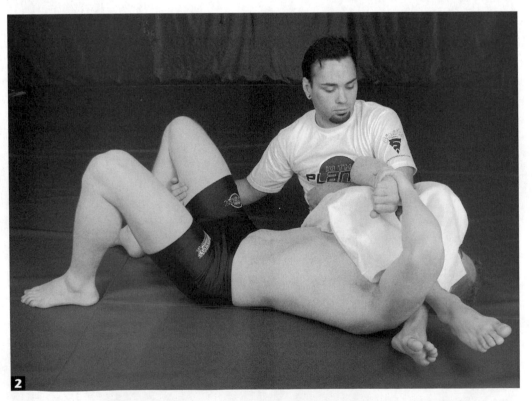

Laurence feels me going for the Arm Crush, so he blocks the move by raising his arms
high. By doing this, however, Laurence has created a gap that allows me to slip my right
foot through his arms and to the left side of his head.

Using my deep under-hook on Laurence's right arm, I fall back and pull Laurence on top of me.

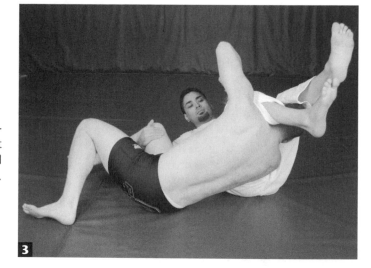

4 (reverse angle) I secure the triangle choke by throwing my left leg over my right foot and squeezing my knees together. Although Laurence is being choked, I can also extend his arm for the arm bar. It's a great move because you can get two submissions at the same time.

The Slide

This is another great submission that can be executed from the Spider Web without letting go of your opponent's right leg. It's rather sly because by leaning back you sometimes trick your opponent into thinking he'll be able to make it up to his knees. But as long as you maintain control of his base with a deep hook around his leg and keep your legs tight against his body, the chances that he'll escape are slim.

I'm ready to attack now that I've swept Laurence into the Spider Web position.

(reverse angle) I fall back, using my left under-hook on Laurence's right arm to pull him with me. At the same time, I'm controlling his right leg to prevent a scramble.

3

(reverse angle) I slide my left arm up to Laurence's right wrist and extend my hips and legs to break his grip.

(reverse angle) Once Laurence's grip is broken, I can sit back for the straight arm bar.

4

X-Break

This is another good technique you can use to break your opponent's grip without letting go of his leg.

I'm ready to attack now that I've swept Laurence into the Spider Web position.

I bring my left leg between Laurence's arms and hook my foot underneath his left arm.

I form an X with my legs by bringing my right leg between Laurence's arms and placing it on top of my left leg.

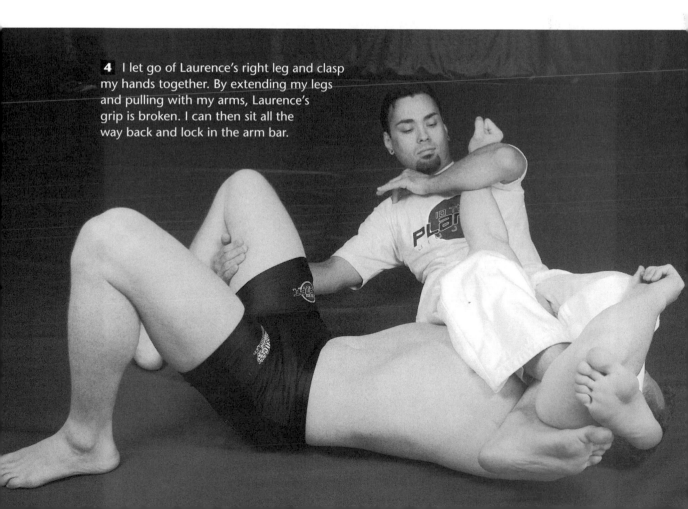

4 I let go of Laurence's right leg and clasp my hands together. By extending my legs and pulling with my arms, Laurence's grip is broken. I can then sit all the way back and lock in the arm bar.

Silverado

Because the Silverado involves letting go of my opponent's leg, giving him a small window of opportunity to escape, it is the last technique I'll go to in order to break my opponent's grip. Although it is a great move to go to if nothing else works, it should be executed as quickly as possible.

I'm ready to attack now that I've swept Laurence into the Spider Web position.

Before I let go of Laurence's right leg, I slide my left arm up to Laurence's wrist to make room for my other arm. Next I let go of Laurence's right leg and press my right elbow into the backside of Laurence's right arm.

3

After locking my hands together in a Gable Grip and squeezing my elbows together, I twist my arms in a counterclockwise motion to break Laurence's grip.

Grabbing Laurence's right wrist with both of my hands, I can now sit back for the straight arm bar.

4

Demonstration of Twister Side Control

3

•••

Twister Side Control

Introduction to Twister Side Control

I learned the Twister during wrestling practice in the ninth grade, but back then I knew it as the Wrestler's Guillotine. It was perhaps the only successful move I acquired during my two years on the mats, and I figured that if it had worked in wrestling, it would most likely work in jiu-jitsu. But it didn't translate as well as I thought. In wrestling, opponents turned their bellies toward the mat and allowed me to take their backs because they didn't want to get their shoulders pinned. That allowed me to climb on top of them, wrap one of their legs between mine, and then roll them over, giving me the Twister. But in jiu-jitsu, nobody gave me their back because it was against jiu-jitsu law.

Not willing to give up on the move, I started searching for ways to set up the Twister from other positions. My instructor Jean Jacques Machado had never before seen the move, and he thought I was crazy. He kept asking me why I was doing that crazy "Twister move." I told him it was called the Wrestler's Guillotine, but apparently he already had the name "Twister" ingrained into his mind. Eventually, he began calling *me* Twister. I would walk into class and he would say, "Hey, how are you doing, Twister?" It drove me crazy—I had been named after a game with a bunch of colored circles.

When I realized that there was no hope of losing the nickname, I made the best of the situation. If I was going to be called the Twister, I'd better find several different setups to be able to pull off in jiu-jitsu. After all, if you have someone's back there is no sense in going for the Twister, not with the rear naked choke right there for the taking. Through much trial and error, I discovered how to get Twister from side control. I managed this by changing angles. Instead of controlling my opponent by laying my torso against his, I'd flip around and control him with my back—a position that I named Twister Side Control. Once I became good at keeping my opponent from escaping, numerous submissions opened up. Usually my opponent would roll into me, trying to capture me in his guard. As he curled his body into me, I would hook his leg, roll him over, and secure the Twister. Or, an opponent might try rolling away from me. I liked that just as well, because then I would follow him over, take his back, and sink in the rear naked choke. If he didn't do anything, just stayed there on his back, I would throw a leg over his body and take the mount. No matter what he tried to do, I almost always came out in a great spot.

Feeling confident pulling the move in the gym, I started trying it in competition and experienced even more success. Those that I trained with every day in the gym learned the hard way about the Twister, and they always had an eye out for it. The opponents I went up against in competition, however, had never seen it before. They knew a hundred little tricks to keep their opponent from securing a submission from traditional side control, but Twister Side Control always threw them for a loop. Before they could figure out what was going on, I was controlling them with my back. They would get rolled, feel a jolt of pain, and tap their hands in submission. I liked the feeling of winning. Knowing it was only a matter of time before people caught on to what I was doing, I kept evolving the Twister Side Control. Soon I would set up the Twister, execute the Twister roll, and then once I was on my back, obtain a position I called The Truck. From there, I could transition right into the Crotch Ripper, Banana Split, or Calf Crank. The possibilities on this revolutionary way to play side control were endless.

Key Concepts

- Twister Side Control is a key position to work from because it opens up submissions that most jiu-jitsu players have never seen or felt.

- The Twister roll takes an acute sense of timing that can only be acquired through thousands of repetitions.

- The Twister moves are very unorthodox, often making them very frustrating to learn. Don't give up. Keep drilling and eventually you'll be landing submissions and setups on your unsuspecting opponents.

The Twister

The longer you spend working from the Twister Side Control position, the more sensitive you'll grow to your opponents' movements. This is important to understand when first trying to execute the Twister submission. As with many moves in this book, it does not come easy. Understanding the timing of when to transition into the Twister roll can take years to master, but once you've got a handle on it, you'll begin tapping out opponents with this unorthodox and flashy submission.

To establish the Twister Side Control position, I place my hips near Joe's right shoulder and lean over his body so that my back is toward his face. My left elbow rests on the mat underneath Joe's left arm. I get close enough to control him, yet still leave enough space so he can turn into me.

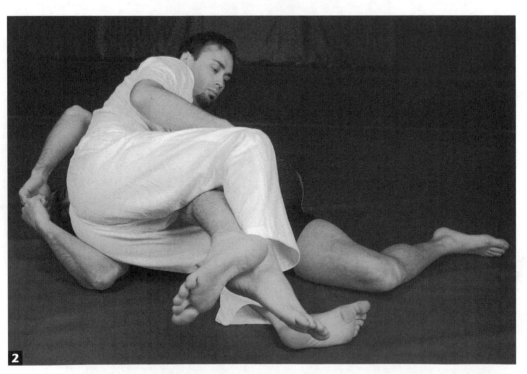

Trying to escape, Joe turns toward me. To capitalize on his movement, I trap his leg by seizing it with both my right leg and right arm.

I secure Joe's leg by bringing my left leg under my right knee in a figure four. To increase the power of my hold, I hook my right foot under Joe's left ankle.

Keeping my weight above Joe's hips, I reach out and grab his right ankle with my right hand.

5

I drop my left shoulder to the mat and roll across my shoulder blades, making sure to keep the figure four tight around Joe's leg.

Once I have Joe on his back, I use my left arm to reach around and under-hook Joe's right arm to prevent him from turning over.

6

As soon as I break Joe's grip, I grab his right wrist with my right hand and guide his arm behind my head.

7

8 I reach under Joe's head with my left arm and over his face with my right arm. Gripping my hands together, I crank his spine by pulling his head toward my body.

The Banana Split

Similar to the Twister, the Banana Split is another classic wrestling move. I don't use it as often as the Twister because most opponents are flexible enough to withstand the pressure being put on their legs. It comes in very handy, however, for those opponents who aren't very limber.

I've established the Twister Side Control position on Joe.

Jiu-Jitsu Unleashed

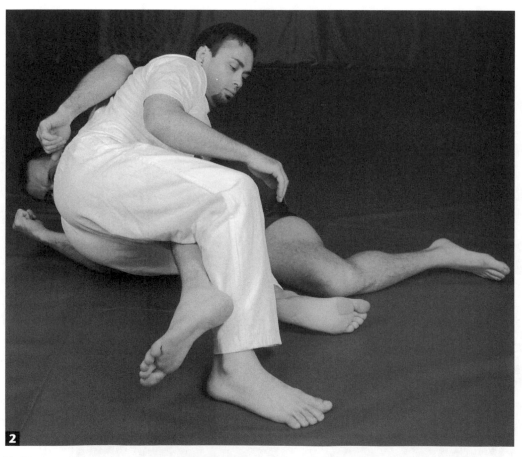

Trying to escape, Joe turns toward me. To capitalize on his movement, I trap his leg by seizing it with both my right leg and right arm.

I secure Joe's leg by bringing my left leg under my right knee in a figure four position. To increase the power of my hold, I hook my right foot under Joe's left ankle.

Keeping my weight above Joe's hips, I reach out and grab his right ankle with my right hand. Then I drop my left shoulder to the mat and roll across my shoulder blades, making sure to keep the figure four tight around Joe's leg.

Once I have Joe on his back, I grab his right ankle with my right hand, while at the same time reaching my left arm around his right leg.

With my right palm facing down, I clasp my hands together using a Gable Grip. I painfully spread Joe's legs by stretching out my legs and pulling with my arms.

The Crotch Ripper

The Crotch Ripper is very similar to the Banana Split, but instead of stretching your opponent's legs apart, you're stretching and twisting your opponent's hips. It's a good submission to know because not many jiu-jitsu players can withstand the pain of this submission. It's also good to know because it doesn't take much energy to execute. Instead of having to use just the strength in your arms and legs, you are using the weight of your whole body, which means that you can pull it off even when fatigued.

I've established the Twister Side Control position on Joe.

2

Trying to escape, Joe turns toward me. To capitalize on his movement, I trap his leg by seizing it with my right leg.

I secure Joe's leg by bringing my left leg under my right knee in a figure four. To increase the power of my hold, I can hook my right foot under Joe's left ankle.

3

Keeping the figure four tight around Joe's left leg, I set up for the Twister roll by reaching under Joe's right leg with my right arm.

Here, as an option, I have chosen to execute the Crotch Ripper from the top position. I achieve this by making a quick Gable Grip around Joe's right leg with my hands, and then using the figure four to stretch out his left leg.

Here I have chosen to go for the Crotch Ripper from the bottom position, so I execute the Twister roll before using the figure four to stretch out Joe's left leg.

The Calf Crank

Once you've set your opponent up for the Twister by trapping his leg and executing the Twister roll, it can sometimes be difficult to get your body into a position where you can reach around his head. If you encounter this problem, there is no need to panic. You can still go for a number of submissions from this control position, which I call The Truck. One of the submissions you can get from The Truck control position is the traditional Calf Crank. If you can't get the Calf Crank, you can resort back to any of the other submissions in this chapter.

Once again, I've established the Twister Side Control position on Joe.

2 Trying to escape, Joe turns toward me. To capitalize on his movement, I trap his leg by seizing it with my right leg.

3

I secure Joe's leg by bringing my left leg under my right knee in a figure four. To increase the power of my hold, I can hook my right foot under Joe's left ankle.

Keeping my weight above Joe's hips, I reach out and grab his right ankle with my right hand. Then I drop my left shoulder to the mat and roll across my shoulder blades, making sure to keep the figure four tight around Joe's leg so he gets rolled over to his back. When Joe is on his back, I grab the top of his left foot with my right hand.

I release the figure four around Joe's left leg. I use my right foot to press my left heel into Joe's leg while pulling down on his foot with my right hand. This puts extreme pressure on Joe's calf muscle.

Kimura Off Twister Side Control

The Kimura is a good option with an opponent who is desperately trying to escape from your Twister Side Control by hooking his left arm around your face. It also works great against opponents who use their left hands to block you from trapping their outside legs. It's a basic counter, but an effective submission hold nonetheless.

I've established Twister Side Control on Joe's right side.

In an attempt to escape, Joe turns toward me while reaching his left arm under my left arm.

Once I feel Joe reach for that under-hook with his left arm, I grab his wrist with my right hand and use my weight to drive his arm down on top of my left arm, pinning his wrist to the mat.

I wrap my left arm underneath Joe's elbow and then grab my right forearm with my left hand. I apply pressure by lifting up with my left arm while pushing down with my right, finishing the Kimura for the submission.

Plan C (Near Arm Bar Off Twister Side Control)

There are only three things your opponent can do when you have established Twister Side Control: turn into you and allow you to get the Twister submission, turn away from you and allow you to take his back, or just lie flat on his back. If your opponent just lies on his back, using his legs to block you from climbing into the mount, you can put your opponent on his side by grabbing his leg closest to you and pinning it to the mat. Doing this allows you to take his arm for the near arm bar.

I've established the Twister Side Control position on Joe's right side.

Joe raises his knee, keeping me from making the transition to the mount, so I use both of my hands to pin Joe's knee to the ground.

Driving my hips forward, I use my weight to roll Joe up on his side.

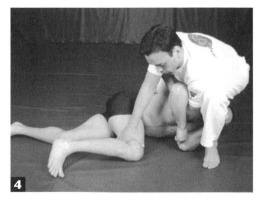

I step forward with my left foot and place my right instep behind Joe's right shoulder. Continuing to press on Joe's right leg with my right hand so he can't turn back toward me, I hook my left arm under his right arm.

To keep Joe from rolling toward me and escaping the submission, I make sure my right instep in under Joe's body. Then I squeeze my knees together and pull his arm toward my chest as I sit back for the straight arm bar.

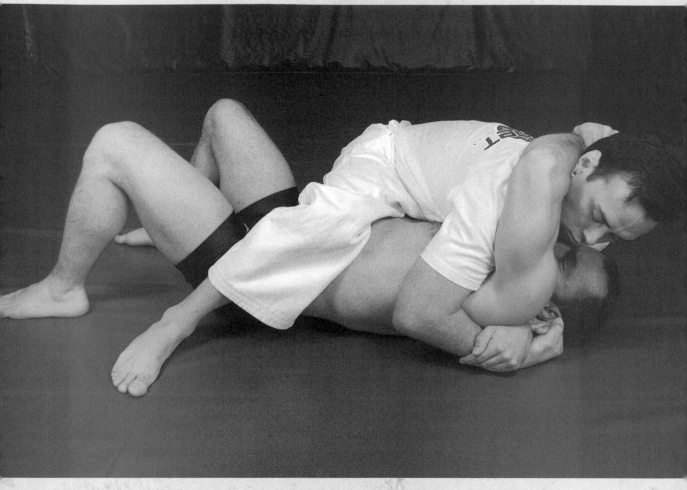

Demonstration of the Mount

4

The Mount

Introduction to the Mount

The first couple of years that I trained in jiu-jitsu, I didn't have much success in the mount. I'd struggle and fight to climb on top of my opponent and achieve what everyone else felt was such a dominant position, but once there, it would only be a matter of seconds until I was bucked off and wind up on my back. After this had happened several hundred times, I began to fear the mount. I thought I was just too light to ever make it work for me. So every time I found myself in side control, instead of trying to set up the mount, which was the traditional route, I'd transition to Twister Side Control.

This worked extremely well in the beginning because once I had Twister Side Control my opponent would either turn into me or away from me. If he turned into me, I would secure the Twister and get him to tap. If he turned away from me, I would take his back and secure a rear naked choke. I was tapping out guys in the gym left and right, but then a few of them began to realize that I despised the mount. Instead of turning into me or away from me, they'd just lie on their backs, not doing anything. They were basically daring me to take the mount because they knew they could buck me off.

Trying to avoid the inevitable, I'd just sit in Twister Side Control, waiting for my opponent to make a move. Sometimes they would, and I'd catch them, but most of the time they would just lie there. Eventually time would run out, and I'd kick myself for being unable to capitalize on such a dominant position. After all, I had no reason not to work on improving my mount. If I got bucked off, usually I'd

123

end up back in the guard and immediately lock my opponent's shoulder and go for an arm bar. If I couldn't get the full guard, I would get half guard and immediately set up the sweep. I was just being lazy, so one day I promised that I would make my mount as effective as my Twister Side Control, if not better.

Before I could work on setting up submissions from the mount, however, I first wanted to learn the best positioning. I asked my teacher Jean Jacques Machado, "If you were mounting the best jiu-jitsu player on the planet, where would your hands be?" He told me that he would put his left arm around his opponent's head and his right arm under his opponent's left arm. When he clasped his hands together, he would control his opponent's head and arm. I knew there were a lot of submissions that you could get when you didn't have the head and arm, but practicing them didn't make sense to me. If having the head and arm was best for control, then that was the position I wanted to base all my submissions off of in the mount. I didn't want to learn submissions off bad positions, just like I hadn't wanted to learn my setups in guard using the gi.

Key Concepts

- Make sure you have a good guard before trying to master the mount. If your guard is dangerous, you'll be more confident on top.

- Take time to work on the mount. It can be extremely frustrating at first because you are always getting rolled, but once you have learned how to establish a good base, the submissions will fall right into place.

- Head and arm control provides the best balance in the mount. If you do not have balance, you don't have offense or defense.

- When your opponent rolls beneath you, learn how to float on top of him to avoid getting pulled to your back.

- When fighting in mixed martial arts (MMA) or in the street, utilizing downward punches from the mount will open up numerous submission possibilities.

Monkey Mount

It didn't take long for me to encounter a problem. Every time I secured my opponent's head and arm, he would reach his hands around my back, lock them together, and hold me down. It stopped me from executing submissions. In order to break my opponent's grip, I tried the traditional route and put my forearm on his throat and pressed down. It worked quite well in the beginning, but eventually my opponents in the gym started to catch on. They began keeping their grips around my back real tight, which kept their entire faces pressed tightly against my chest, leaving no room for me to wedge my elbow down into their throats.

I began experimenting. With both of my hands already locked together, there wasn't much I could do with them. So, I decided to use my feet. If I had my left arm hooked under my opponent's head, I could place my right foot on his hip. I used that base to push my weight into his left shoulder, stretching him out and breaking his lock around my back. I also discovered that placing my foot on my opponent's hip acted as a cushion. When my opponent bridged or tried bucking me off, I would immediately feel it and be able to put my legs down to serve as a base. The position worked so well, I gave it a name, Monkey Mount, and started hunting for submissions.

Eddie in the Monkey Mount

Slow Triangle

Although triangle cshokes can be set up several different ways from the mount, such as baiting your opponent by going for an arm bar, I recommend using the Slow Triangle setup first. As with most of my setups, it revolves around head and arm control, which allows you to stay tight to your opponent and to make smooth transitions.

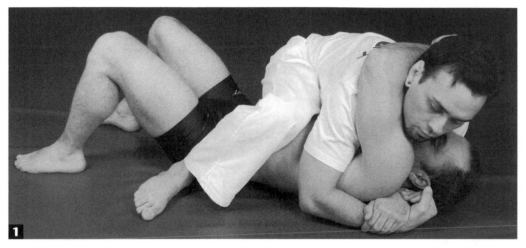

It's important to notice how I've mounted Joe. I've placed my left knee up by his right armpit. I've wrapped my left arm underneath his head and my right arm under his left arm, locking my hands together to secure head and arm control.

Knowing I need to break Joe's grip, I place my right foot on Joe's left hip and push off of it. This drives my shoulders forward and down to the mat, forcing Joe's arms apart.

3 I grab hold of Joe's left wrist with my right hand, using my weight to help me pin it to the mat.

While keeping Joe's left arm pinned to the mat, I slip my right foot through the gap and grab hold of my ankle with my left hand.

I use my left hand to snake my leg underneath Joe's head. While doing this, I keep his left arm pinned to the mat so he can't use it to fend off the hook.

I bring my left leg over my right. Squeezing my knees together and pulling up on Joe's head, I lock in the triangle choke.

Arm Triangle

Although arm triangles can be utilized from a number of different positions, they work best from the mount because you can use your weight to help lock in the choke.

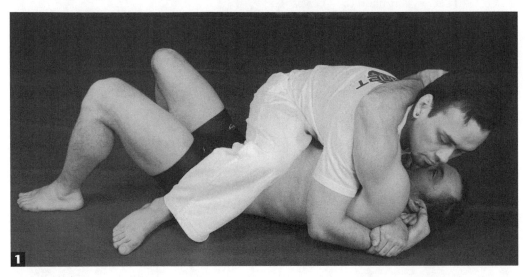

I've established the mount on Joe.

By placing my right foot on Joe's left hip and pushing off, I drive my shoulders forward and down to the mat, breaking Joe's arms apart. As I do this, I release the head and arm, maintaining control by gripping under Joe's left shoulder with my left hand.

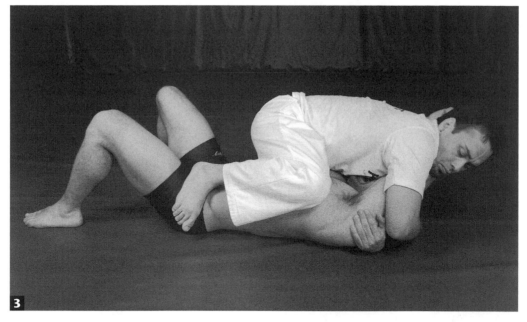

Once I have broken Joe's grip, I shift my weight to the left, using my right arm to help guide Joe's arm to the left side of my head. To ensure this goes smoothly, I continue to grip Joe's left shoulder with my left hand.

I use my head to press Joe's arm into his neck.

I place my left hand on my right bicep and my right hand on my right ear. As I squeeze my arms together, I post on my right leg and drive my left knee down in to Joe's stomach. I finish the choke by driving my weight forward and down.

Inverted Arm Bar

No-gi grappling can be slippery due to all the sweat, which adds some difficulty when trying to pull off an Inverted Arm Bar. To prevent your opponent from slipping out of the hold, it is best to transition into the move immediately after you break your opponent's grip.

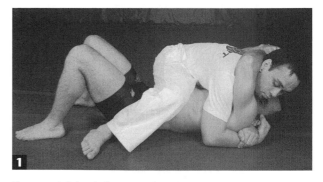

I've established the mount on Joe.

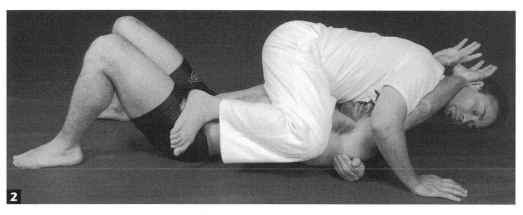

By placing my right foot on Joe's left hip and pushing off, I drive my shoulders forward and down to the mat, breaking Joe's arms apart. As I do this, I release the head and arm, maintaining control by gripping under Joe's left shoulder with my left hand.

After I break Joe's grip, I wrap my right arm underneath Joe's left arm, and then clasp my hands together using a Gable Grip, making sure my right palm is facing down. With my right arm positioned just below Joe's left elbow, I pull up with both arms. At the same time, I use my shoulder to drive the top of Joe's arm down. Joe, feeling his arm hyperextending, taps his hand in submission.

Arm Bar from the Mount

Arm bars frequently present themselves from the mount, especially when your opponent makes a mistake, but just as in the guard, it's important not to jump right into them. By making a smooth transition to Spider Web, you can control your opponent as he tries to scramble for an escape. After examining all your options, you can then go for the arm bar.

I've established the mount on Joe.

By placing my right foot on Joe's left hip and pushing off, I drive my shoulders forward and down to the mat, breaking Joe's arms apart. As I do this, I release the head and arm, maintaining control by gripping under Joe's left shoulder with my left hand.

Just as I did when setting up the Slow Triangle, I use my right hand and the weight of my body to pin Joe's left arm to the mat.

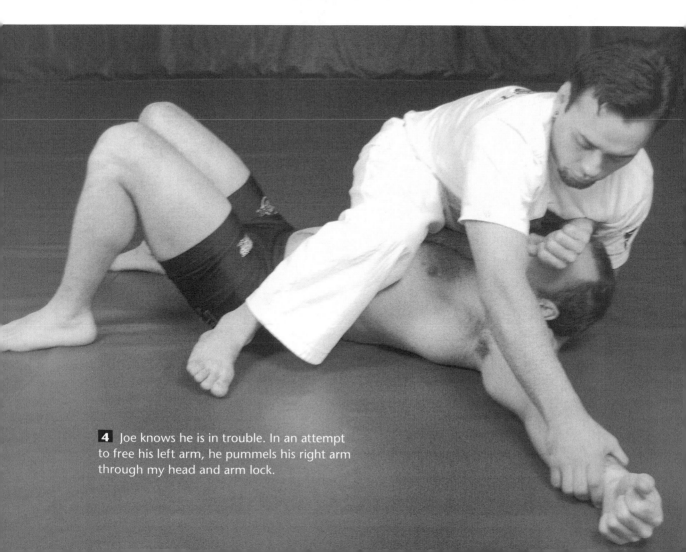

3

4 Joe knows he is in trouble. In an attempt to free his left arm, he pummels his right arm through my head and arm lock.

Once I feel him do this, I release his left hand and hook his right arm with my left arm. Then I fall back, reaching under Joe's right leg with my right arm.

I throw my left leg over Joe's head and cross my feet, securing the Spider Web position.

Loco Plata

Once you've secured the head and arm while in the mount, sometimes your opponent will sneak his arm through your lock to get the double under-hooks. If this happens, the Loco Plata is a great move to use. It's set up a lot like the Go-Go Plata from the guard, only you are doing it from the mount.

I've established the mount, but Joe sneaked his arm through my head and arm control and now he has double under-hooks.

First I need to break Joe's grip, which I accomplish by driving my right forearm across his neck.

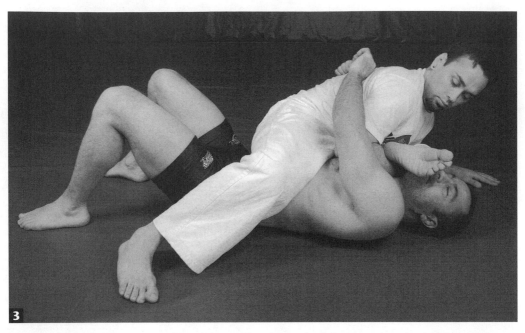

Now that I've broken Joe's grip, I shift my weight to the left. Then I under-hook my left ankle with my right wrist and bring it up toward Joe's head. As I do this, I post on my left arm for balance.

While trapping Joe's right arm in my left armpit, I slide my left foot over Joe's neck and push down on it with my right hand.

5

I reach around Joe's head with my left arm and grab the top of my left foot. At the same time, I put my right foot on top of my left heel and drive down, locking in the neck crank submission.

Eddie in Back Control

5

...

The Back

Introduction to the Back

While executing the Twister roll, I knew that the opportunity to take my opponent's back was just one step away. Most jiu-jitsu players would jump at such an option, but I had the Twister. I thought it wise to stick with a proven submission rather than transition into what I considered a weaker position. But eventually I was forced to rethink my strategy. I used the Twister so much that some of the top jiu-jitsu players at Jean Jacques Machado's Academy started getting wise. After performing the Twister roll, they would hide their right arms, which I needed in order to slap on the Twister. They basically gave me their backs by doing this, so I had two options. Stalemate or take their backs. I started taking their backs, and that's when I realized just how much work I had ahead of me.

I didn't want to be just OK at the back, not after I had done all that work to set my opponent up in the Twister, so I began breaking the position down. I realized that when he wore a gi, I could control my opponent by hooking my legs underneath him the traditional way. But when my opponent didn't wear a gi, due to all the sweat, he could easily slip and slide underneath me, often flipping over and putting me back into my guard. I wanted to master grappling for mixed martial arts (MMA) competition, so it didn't make sense to control my opponent the traditional way. To solve the problem, I watched many fight tapes of Jean Jacques competing in Abu Dhabi. When he took an opponent's back, he would wrap his legs around his opponent's midsection using a triangle configuration. He cinched it down so tight it made it impossible for his opponent to spin and gain a more favorable position. I decided to adopt the move, which I call the Anaconda. But getting it wasn't easy. Giving up your back was one of the biggest no-no's in jiu-jitsu, so competitors always put up a fight to stop me from getting my hooks locked in. At times it felt like I was riding a wild bull, and I was getting bucked off more than I liked. Eventually I realized that the process of locking my legs around my opponent's torso would be much easier if I first controlled his upper body.

There were really only three ways to do that. The double under-hooks worked well on an opponent wearing a gi because after reaching my hands under my opponent's arms I could grab their collars to hold the under-hooks in place. The double under-hooks, however, didn't work so well when my opponent wasn't wearing a gi because there was nothing to hold on to and my opponent could over-hook my arm and lock in the Kimura. I could use double over-hooks and immediately go for the choke, but if I didn't have the Anaconda locked down I would lose control of my opponent.

Most experienced competitors knew all sorts of tricks to defend against the choke—such as tucking their chin or bucking like a madman—and usually they'd squirm away before I could lock one in. The last option seemed to work the best—over-hook with one arm and under-hook with the other. Once I'd clasped my hands together using a Gable Grip, I'd squeeze into my opponent's chest to hold him firmly in place so I could lock in the Anaconda. Only after his lower body was trapped in my vise would I go for the choke.

Once I had the system worked out, I went for it all the time. The moment an opponent gave me his back, I would slide one arm over and one under while still on my knees, lock my hands together and squeeze into his midsection, climb on top of his back to lock in the Anaconda, and then go for the choke. Although it was often difficult to climb on top and secure the Anaconda, as long as I had the over-hook and under-hook locked together with a Gable Grip, I could ride out his thrashing. With this system, it didn't take long to become an expert bull rider.

Key Concepts

- The back is not only one of the hardest positions to obtain, but it is also one of the hardest positions to keep.

- To get and keep your opponent's back you must follow these steps as if they were law:

  1. After establishing an over-under hook body lock with your arms, clasp your hands together using a Gable Grip and squeeze tightly into the center of your opponent's chest.

  2. Working to get your hooks in can be difficult. Use your lock to throw your opponent off balance and create space to get your hooks in.

  3. Once you have your hooks in, go right to the Anaconda (a figure four) with your legs. Securing the Anaconda will greatly restrict your opponent's ability to turn. By cinching down with the Anaconda, you can also restrict your opponent's breathing and distract him from the chokehold.

  4. From here you can start the hand fight and work for the choke.

Basic Rear Naked Choke

The whole reason for taking an opponent's back is to sink in the rear naked choke. Although it can be a battle to get it, once you have all your limbs in the proper positions, it doesn't take much to make it work.

1

Once I've secured an over-under body lock around Laurence's back using a Gable Grip, I squeeze my hands tight into his chest.

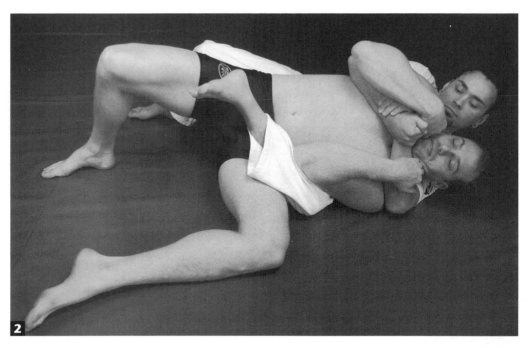

Using the over-under body lock to pull Laurence with me as I fall back, I work to get my hooks in, sliding my left leg over Laurence's left hip.

After bringing my left leg across Laurence's body, I throw my right leg over my left leg in a figure four position, locking in the Anaconda.

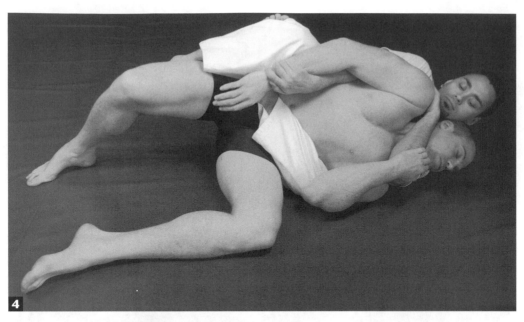

With the Anaconda locked in, I don't have to worry about Laurence turning toward me, so I can start the hand fight. I grab Laurence's right wrist with my right hand and pin it down by his waist. Now that Laurence's right arm is out of the picture, I grip his right shoulder with my left hand and start inching my forearm toward his throat.

As soon as I get my left arm deep around Laurence's neck, I release his right arm and quickly bring my right arm up, sliding it behind Laurence's head. To finish the choke, I place my left hand on my right bicep and squeeze, strangling Laurence until he taps or passes out.

The 100 Percent

The 100 Percent can be set up from a couple of different positions, but the most common is when your opponent shoots in to seize your legs. If you are able to stop the shot and get the proper hooks with your arms, you should be able to pull this move off 100 percent of the time.

Laurence shoots in for the takedown and I sprawl, catching him on my left hip. I reach under his right arm with my left hand, and then clasp my hands together underneath his armpit using a Gable Grip.

I throw my right leg under Laurence. Then using my weight and the tight body lock, I pull Laurence over to his back.

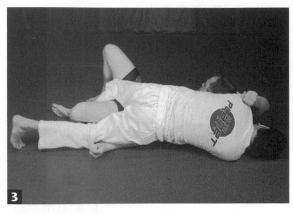

3

I hook my left leg around Laurence's left leg so he can't use our current momentum to roll me onto my back.

4

Laurence is still trying to roll away from me, so I come up to my right knee and use the hook around his leg as well as the body lock to pull him back toward me (see below).

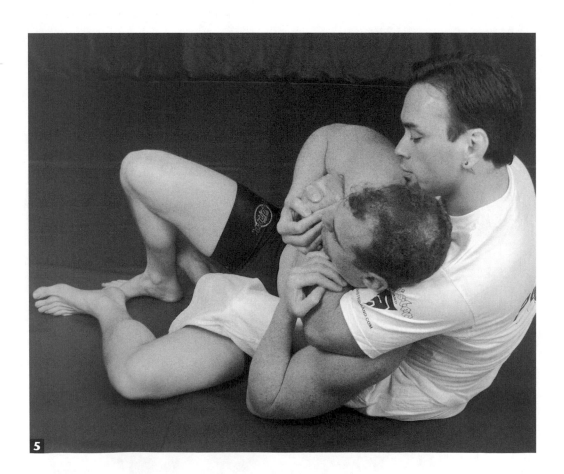

5

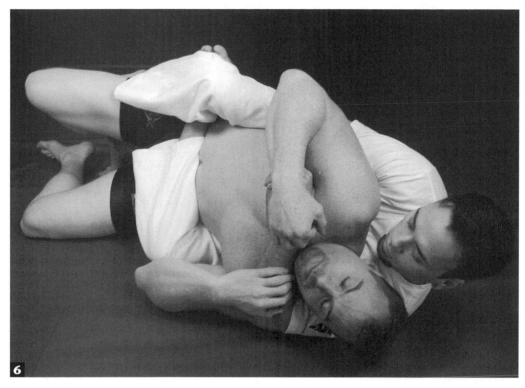

6

After bringing my left leg across Laurence's body, I throw my right leg over my left foot in a figure four position, locking in the Anaconda.

7

8

With the Anaconda locked in, I don't have to worry about Laurence turning toward me. I start the hand fight by grabbing Laurence's right wrist with my right hand and pinning it down by his waist. Now that Laurence's right arm is out of the picture, I grip his right shoulder with my left hand and start inching my forearm toward his throat.

As soon as I get my left arm deep around Laurence's neck, I release his right arm and quickly bring my right arm up, sliding it behind Laurence's head. To finish the choke, I place my left hand on my right bicep and squeeze, strangling Laurence until he taps.

Marcelo

This move is an effective way of taking the back, made famous by a jiu-jitsu fighter named Marcelo Garcia. It should be executed explosively, requiring a considerable amount of control when making the transition to the back.

Laurence shoots in to seize my legs for a takedown, but I'm able to sprawl my legs back and stop him from accomplishing his goal. To gain head and arm control, I reach over his left shoulder with my right arm and under his left shoulder with my left arm, locking my hands together using a Gable Grip.

In one rapid cartwheel-like motion, I jump on Laurence's back and hook my right leg under his right leg.

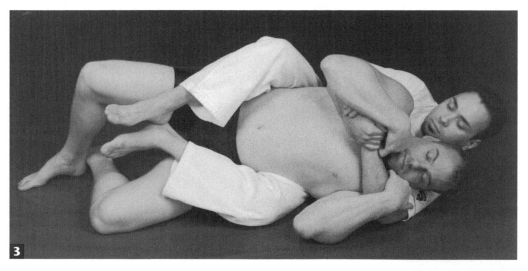

I use my right hook along with the power of the over-under body lock to force Laurence in a clockwise direction, putting him on his side. During the transition, I manage to hook my left leg over Laurence's left leg.

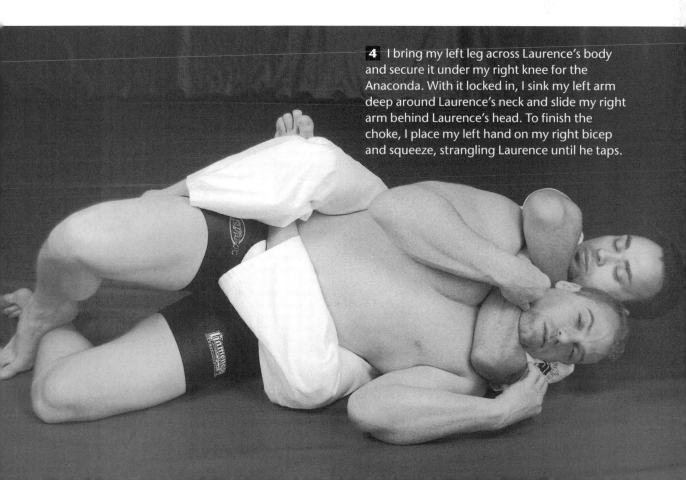

4 I bring my left leg across Laurence's body and secure it under my right knee for the Anaconda. With it locked in, I sink my left arm deep around Laurence's neck and slide my right arm behind Laurence's head. To finish the choke, I place my left hand on my right bicep and squeeze, strangling Laurence until he taps.

6

◆◆◆

Passing the Guard

Introduction to Passing the Guard

Although there are submissions you can utilize when you're in your opponent's guard or half guard, there are a lot more submissions that you can attempt while in the side control or the mount positions. So when you are in your opponent's guard or half guard, the ultimate goal is to set up a pass to get to one of these superior positions.

I wasn't very adept at setting up and executing passes early in my jiu-jitsu career, but I felt that with my system of half guard sweeps, I didn't really need to be. Most of the time I would pull my opponent into *my* half guard or guard, and from there I would sweep him over to his back. Instead of falling into my opponent's half guard or guard as most players did, I would use the momentum of the sweep to immediately pass into side control. I designed all my sweeps with passes at the end, and I'd do them quickly, before my opponent had a chance to recover from the sweep. It saved me from having to set up a pass all on its own.

I thought my strategy was flawless until I went up against a famous mixed martial arts (MMA) fighter in a jiu-jitsu tournament. I was stuck in his guard for a large part of the match, and because I had designed all my passes off sweeps from my half guard, I didn't know what to do. It's not that he was so good that passing his guard was simply impossible. He was playing open guard with his legs spread wide, basically giving me the underpass, the first pass explained in this chapter. I just hadn't practiced the underpass enough to be able to pull it off, so I lost the match.

It angered me that I lost because I wasn't skilled enough at a certain move. I promised myself that if I ever went up against that MMA fighter again, I would have the underpass mastered. So I went to Jean Jacques Machado, who is the king of passing, and he broke it down for me move by move, which is exactly how I teach it to my students. I drilled it for six solid months, day after day, until I felt I could pass anyone's full guard. Then I went down to the MMA fighter's school to see if I could actually pull it off. We rolled for a few minutes, and then he started playing open guard, giving me the underpass. I had practiced it so much I pulled it off without even thinking, and I caught him in the Banana Split, forcing him to tap.

Although I had been redeemed, I realized that just as with every other technique, the underpass wasn't going to work all the time. Every opponent reacts and moves differently, so in order to truly master passing my opponent's guard, I had to know a variety of passes. Consequently, I began breaking down the dynamics of passing. I learned that there were a lot of fancy moves that could be executed while grappling with a gi, such as grabbing the pants leg of your opponent's uni-

form and tossing him aside, but I didn't want to learn how to pass while wearing a gi. I wanted to learn the best passes for MMA competition, which meant that there were fewer options. You couldn't hover above your opponent, waiting for an opening to present itself, because you'd get punched in the face. In MMA, you either had to be right on top of your opponent or far enough away that you couldn't get kicked in the face or knees.

As I discovered, there are a handful of passes that translate beautifully to MMA competition, and these are the ones that I have described in this chapter. Once you learn them, it might seem as if you don't have many options. All I can tell you is to keep practicing. After you've rolled with half a dozen different opponents, you'll begin to realize that passing isn't an exact science. Your opponent is going to scramble, so to make the passes described here successful, you are going to have to alter them slightly to fit the situation. The important thing is for you to practice and drill, tweaking the moves so they work best for you. If you can't jump the fence into side mount or mount, you can't rob the house.

Key Concepts

- If you are training for MMA competition, be sure to stay tight to your opponent when making these passes to avoid getting punched.

- Passing is 80 percent scrambling. Sometimes you're going to get the pass just as shown here, but most of the time you will have to adjust your pass to the scramble in order to reach the finish line.

- If one pass doesn't work, move right to the next. Keep going back and forth until you're successful. Eventually your opponent will slip and you will get the pass.

The Underpass

The Underpass was the first effective pass that I learned to escape the full guard, and I still use it quite often because it works well for both no-gi grappling and MMA competition. It's a rather basic technique, but that doesn't mean you can practice it once or twice and expect to use it in competition. In order to be effective with any technique, you must drill it repeatedly with a variety of opponents to get a feel for how the various body types move and react.

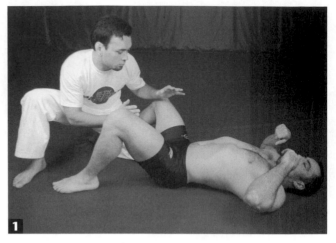

I'm in Joe's open guard.

As I snake both of my arms underneath Joe's legs and clasp my hands together above his stomach using a Gable Grip, I press forward and lift Joe's hips off the mat.

Throwing my legs back and shifting my weight in a clockwise direction, I drive my left hand down to Joe's shoulder while continuing to control his hips with my right hand.

Pressing all my weight down onto Joe, I clear his legs and move into side control.

Staple Gun

The Staple Gun is a pass that should be utilized when your opponent is able to get a leg on the inside of your hip (Butterfly Hook), making it so you can only under-hook one of his legs. The pass complements the underpass. If you are unable to go to the Underpass, go right to the Staple Gun. If you're unable to secure the Staple Gun, go right back to the Underpass. These passes work so beautifully together that I use them as my base for passing the full guard.

I'm in Joe's open guard.

I reach under Joe's legs just as I did in the Underpass, only Joe was able to maneuver his right leg to the inside of my right hip. Although I still have Joe's left leg hooked, I need to make sure Joe's right leg is trapped so he can't swing it around my head and secure a triangle choke.

I place my right leg on top of Joe's right leg, pinning it to the ground. While staying tight to Joe's body, I then bring my left knee up to Joe's right hip.

Keeping my right hook around Joe's left leg to prevent a scramble, I back-step out into Twister Side Control.

Tornado

The Staple Gun is slow and methodical, breaking down your opponent's guard step-by-step. The Tornado is an explosive move executed at high speed. Instead of putting you in side control as will both the Staple Gun and the Underpass, the Tornado will usually only get you to half guard. Although this isn't as preferable, getting to your opponent's half guard is still a success. Once there, you can utilize one of the other passes described in this chapter to transition to side mount or mount.

Again, I'm in Joe's open guard.

I step into Joe's guard, under-hooking his left leg with my right arm while controlling his right leg with my left arm.

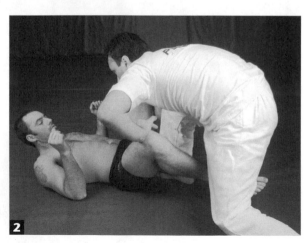

I use my left hand to push Joe's right knee in as I explode past his guard by spinning in a clockwise motion. Making sure to keep my under-hook on Joe's left leg, I back-step into Twister Side Control.

Twister Pass

If you are able to pull off the Tornado, but you end up facing your opponent's legs in the half guard, go right into the Twister Pass. This move can be tricky to control because you're giving your opponent your back, but if you have already become comfortable in the Twister Side Control position, then the move will feel natural.

I just passed Joe's full guard utilizing the Tornado, but he was able to catch my right leg and put me in his half guard. In an attempt to free my leg, I sit out so my back is facing Joe's head and use my right hand to push on Joe's left knee.

I bring my left leg under Joe's legs and hook his left ankle to help break the Lockdown. As I do this, I continue to push on Joe's knee with my right hand.

3

Once I break Joe's legs by pushing with my right hand, I get enough separation to free my leg and back-step into Twister Side Control.

4

No-Hand Pass

This is one of the few passes that works well for gi grappling, as well as no-gi grappling and MMA. It is basic, but highly effective and hard to stop. If done correctly, the No-Hand Pass will take you right into the side control or mount. Before attempting it, however, it is important to have your opponent in head and arm control. This takes away your opponent's under-hook and makes his half guard very limited.

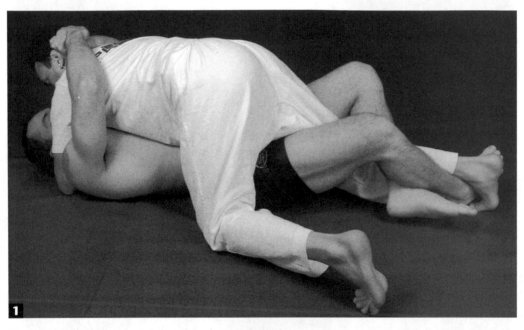

I'm in Joe's half guard with head and arm control.

To start the pass, I bring my left leg up and hook the top of my foot above Joe's right knee.

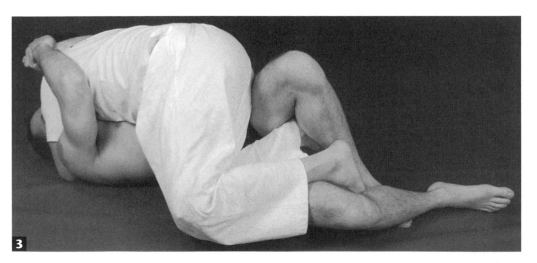

I use my hook to push down on Joe's knee, breaking his Lockdown on my right leg.

4 Using my left leg to pin Joe's right leg to the ground, I create enough room to slide my right knee over Joe's right leg. Once past Joe's guard, I make the transition into the side control position.

7

•••

Transitions

Introduction to Transitions

Jiu-jitsu can often seem like nothing more than a frenzy of moves, two fighters rolling around haphazardly in an attempt to gain the most advantageous position. Scrambling is a big part of jiu-jitsu, and although it is important to learn how to hold a position to lock in finishing holds, it's equally important to understand how to make transitions from one position to the next in the heat of the scramble.

After wrestling with the same opponents day in and day out, your favorite techniques will eventually become ineffective. If you are a master of the guard, your sparring partners will soon learn how to counter every move that you attempt from the guard. In order to escape these stalemates, you must learn various ways to move from one position to the next so you can try new submissions. If the guard isn't working, you can jump over to Twister Side Control. If you have no success in Twister Side Control, you can jump over to the mount. This forces you to evolve, to break down and master every position, not just your favorite ones. Although every transition will change depending on your opponent's body type and movement, to help you get started, this chapter lists a few basic transitions from each of the core positions presented previously in this book.

Ninja: Twister Side Control to Back Control

The Ninja is a move that I developed for opponents who became very good at defending the Twister. There were a couple of guys I grappled with on a regular basis who knew my signature move inside and out, so if I had any doubts about being able to catch them in the Twister, I'd switch things up and pull out the Ninja. I like it because it takes you from the Twister roll to your opponent's back to an over-under hook all in one motion. And if done properly, you come off looking like a Ninja.

I've established the Twister Side Control position on Laurence.

Trying to escape, Laurence turns toward me. To capitalize on his movement, I trap his leg by seizing it with both my right leg and right arm.

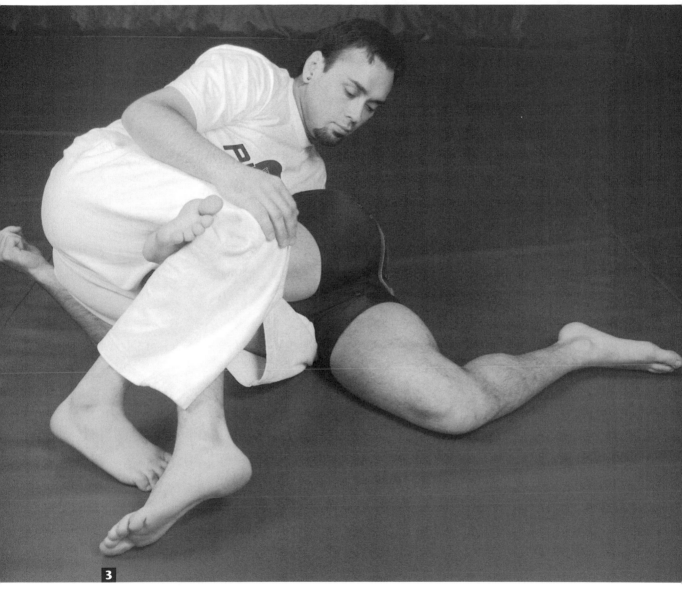

3

I secure Laurence's leg by bringing my left leg under my right knee in a figure four. To increase the power of my hold, I can hook my right foot under Laurence's left ankle.

Keeping my weight above Laurence's hips, I reach out and grab his right ankle with my right hand. Then I drop my left shoulder to the mat and roll across my shoulder blades, making sure to keep the figure four tight around Laurence's leg so he gets rolled over to his back.

As soon as I roll Laurence onto his back, I reach around his head with my left arm and under his right arm with my right arm, locking my hands together using a Gable Grip.

7 I release Laurence's left leg by bringing my left leg across his stomach. I place my left foot under my right knee, cinching in the Anaconda. From here I can proceed with the hand fight and work for the rear naked choke.

Twister Side Control to Back Control: Option 2

This transition to the back off Twister Side Control should be used when your opponent is just lying on his back, blocking you from climbing into the mount with his knee.

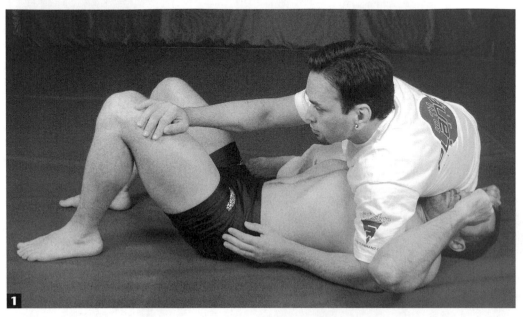

I've established the Twister Side Control position on Laurence's right side. Laurence keeps his knees high to stop me from making the transition to the mount.

I use both of my hands to pin Laurence's knee to the ground.

3

I sprawl back, wrapping my right arm under Laurence's right arm and my left arm over his left shoulder. I clasp my hands together using a Gable Grip.

4

I use my over-under lock to pull Laurence into me as I sit back. As I do this, I throw my right leg across Laurence's stomach and work to get my left leg under his body.

5

Continuing to use the power of the over-under lock to rotate Laurence to my right, I get my left leg all the way under and around Laurence's body so I can place it over my right foot. Once I have the Anaconda locked in, I can work to get the choke.

Detour to Back: Spider Web to Back Control

This move should be used when you're almost in the Spider Web position but your right leg is trapped under your opponent's ribs. When in this situation, many jiu-jitsu players' first instincts will be to sit back for the arm bar anyway, but this is risky because there is a big opening that gives your opponent a chance to escape. A better option is to complete the Spider Web position by getting your right leg across your opponent's body. But if your opponent just isn't letting you do that or there's not enough room, transitioning to the back can be your safest option.

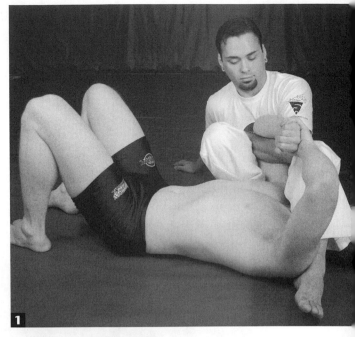

I've got Laurence partially in the Spider Web position, only my right leg is stuck under his ribs.

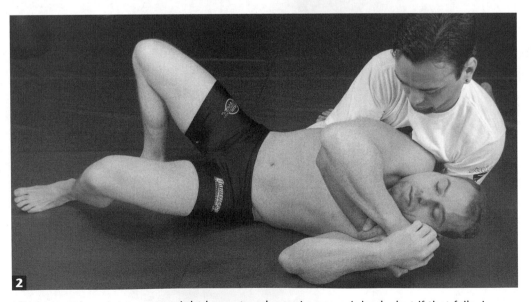

I first try and work to get my right leg out and over Laurence's body, but if that fails, I immediately start to make the transition to the back. I do this by sprawling back and wrapping my left arm around his left shoulder and my right arm under his right arm. I clasp my hands together using a Gable Grip.

I use the over-under lock to pull Laurence into me as I sit up. As I do this, I throw my right leg across his stomach and work to get my left leg under his body.

3

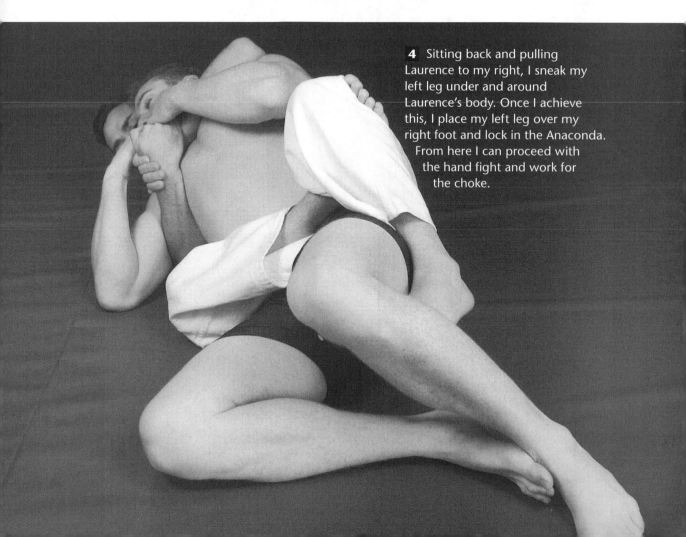

4 Sitting back and pulling Laurence to my right, I sneak my left leg under and around Laurence's body. Once I achieve this, I place my left leg over my right foot and lock in the Anaconda. From here I can proceed with the hand fight and work for the choke.

Back to the Twister

This is a move that should be executed when you just aren't having any luck with your opponent's back. If your opponent is winning the hand battle or is an expert at defending the choke, sometimes it's better to make a quick transition to the Twister rather than stay and fight. Going from the back to the Twister and vice versa are the easiest transitions to make. From either position, you're just one hook away from making the change.

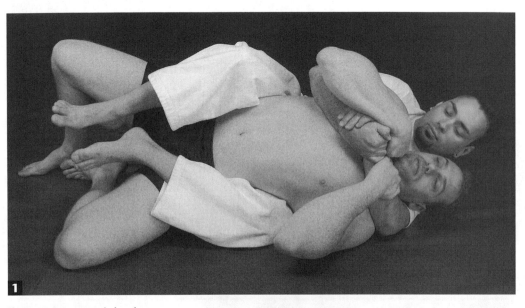

I've got Laurence's back.

I release my right hook and sneak my left leg between Laurence's legs, cinching in the Lockdown on his left leg. As I do this, I use my over-under lock to control his upper body.

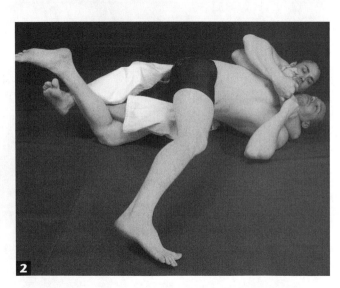

I let go of the over-under lock and hook my right arm underneath Laurence's right arm. This will stop him from spinning away from me.

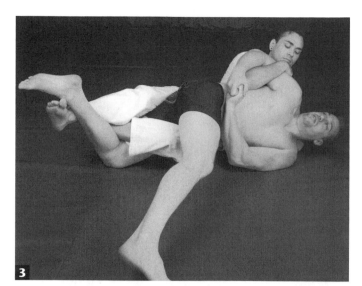

After I sneak my left arm underneath Laurence's right arm, I take my right arm out and clasp my hands together to help break Laurence's grip.

5

Once I break Laurence's grip, I work to get my left arm around the back of his head.

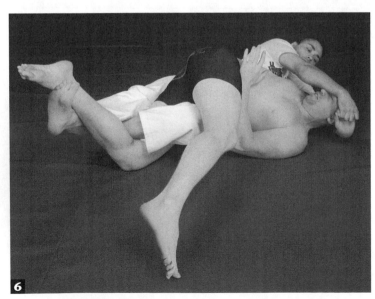

I can now reach over Laurence's face with my right arm. Gripping my hands together, I crank his spine by pulling his head toward my body.

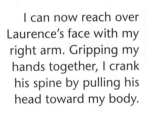

6

Swim Move: Invisible Collar to Spider Web

The Swim move takes your opponent from your guard, puts him on his back, and then lands him in your Spider Web. In this sequence I've gone through all the steps: starting from Mission Control, going to the New York, and then moving into the Invisible Collar where I start the transition into Spider Web.

I've got Laurence in the Invisible Collar.

I push Laurence's right arm across my body using my left hand.

As I hook my left arm through Laurence's right arm and grab my right hip, I turn to my right side.

I swivel my hips out so that my belly is on the mat.

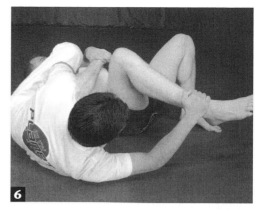

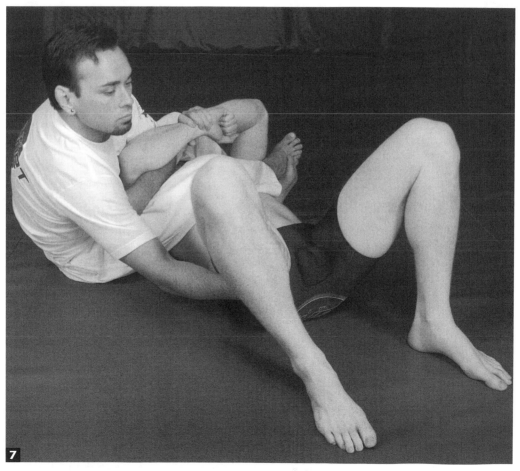

I keep rotating, grabbing Laurence's right ankle with my right hand to help me roll him over to his back. Once Laurence is on his back, I can attack from the Spider Web position.

The Creep: Back to Spider Web

Here is another great transition that takes you from back control to the Spider Web position.

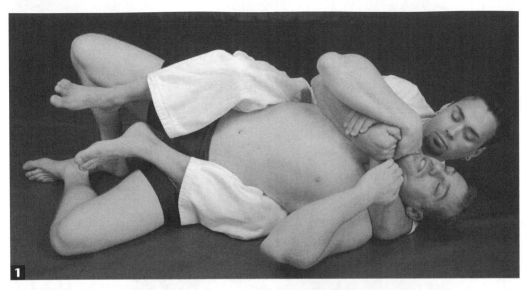

I've got Laurence's back.

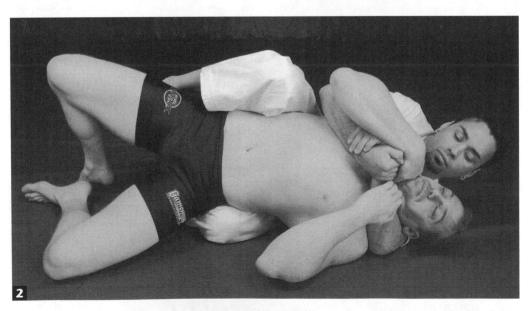

After wrapping my left arm over Laurence's left shoulder and my right arm under his right arm, I throw my right leg behind Laurence and use it to push on his right hip. As I do this, I work to get my left leg out from underneath him.

Once I'm able to get my left leg out from underneath Laurence's body, I throw my right leg across his stomach. I make sure to keep my over-under lock tight around his body as I do this.

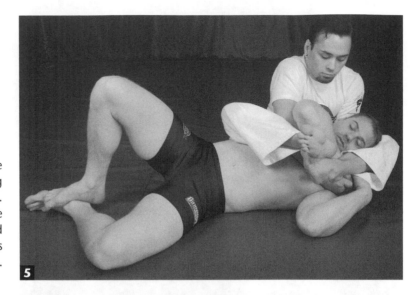

I pull Laurence toward me using my over-under lock. As I do this, I snake my left leg around his head and cross my feet.

5

6

I reach back and secure Laurence's right leg with my right hand to prevent a scramble. At the same time, I maneuver my left leg over Laurence's head and my left arm underneath his right arm. Now I can work to attack his arm from the Spider Web position.

Index